BFI Film Classics

The BFI Film Classics is a series of books that introduces, interprets and celebrates landmarks of world cinema. Each volume offers an argument for the film's 'classic' status, together with discussion of its production and reception history, its place within a genre or national cinema, an account of its technical and aesthetic importance, and in many cases, the author's personal response to the film.

'Magnificently concentrated examples of flowing freeform critical poetry.'
Uncut

'A formidable body of work collectively generating some fascinating insights into the evolution of cinema.'
Times Higher Education Supplement

'The definitive film companion essays.'
Hotdog

'The series is a landmark in film criticism.'
Quarterly Review of Film and Video

City Lights

Charles Maland

First published in 2007 by the
British Film Institute
21 Stephen Street, London W1T 1LN

Copyright © Charles Maland 2007

The British Film Institute promotes greater understanding and
appreciation of, and access to, film and moving image culture in
the UK.

British Library Cataloguing-in-Publication Data
A catalogue record for this book is available from the British Library

ISBN 978-1-84457-175-8

Cover Design by Ashley Western
Series text design: ketchup/SE14

Typeset by D R Bungay Associates, Burghfield, Berks
Printed in the UK by Cromwell Press, Trowbridge, Wiltshire

Contents

Acknowledgments

When Alex Haley was a Visiting Professor at the University of Tennessee, I heard him say several times that if you find a turtle atop a fence post, you know someone helped him get there. Writing a book is always a more communal enterprise than one might expect, and writing this book has been a particular pleasure for me, not least because of the generosity and assistance of those who have helped me along the way. *City Lights* has brought out the best in people.

Thanks first to those who helped me explore the plethora of documents related to *City Lights*: Kate Guyonvarch and her assistant Claire Byrski at Association Chaplin in Paris; Cecilia Cenciarielli, Curator and Head of Progetto Chaplin, and her staff, particularly Michela Zegna, at the Cineteca di Bologna; Gian Luca Farinelli, Director of the Cineteca; archivist Evelyne Lüthi-Graf and her assistant Eléanore Rinaldi at the Archives de Montreux; Barbara Hall at the Margaret Herrick Library; Janet Lorenz at the National Film Information Service; and the entire staffs of the Circulation and Interlibrary Loan Departments at the John C. Hodges Library at the University of Tennessee, my wonderful home library.

A number of film scholars and experts on Chaplin and his films have been kind enough to share their expertise with me and offer their assistance in various ways. Deepest appreciation to John Bengston, Tom Doherty, Mike Hammond, Richard Jewell, Dan Kamin, Richard Maltby, Bonnie McCourt, Hooman Mehran, David Robinson, Frank Scheide, Lisa Stein, David Totheroh, and last but certainly not least, Jeffrey Vance. Composer Timothy Brock was generous with his time and genial about my minimal musical knowledge; his tutelage deeply enhanced my understanding and appreciation of the *City Lights* score, especially in the final scene. Although I bear responsibility for what appears here, they have made this a better book.

At the BFI I would like to thank all who helped see the production through, particularly editors Rebecca Barden and Sarah Watt, editorial production manager Tom Cabot, and the three anonymous readers who read my draft manuscript with care and offered useful suggestions for this final version.

The University of Tennessee has provided me with institutional support and a nurturing intellectual community for over two decades. The Office of Research, College of Arts and Sciences, and the John C. Hodges Fund all contributed travel and research assistance for this project. I'd like to offer a collective thanks to my colleagues, current and emeritus, in the English Department, Cinema Studies, and American Studies, as well as to my graduate and undergraduate students in film studies. More particularly, I'd like to thank Department Head John Zomchick for supporting the project; Mary Papke, for reading and commenting on an earlier draft; and Chris Holmlund, Bill Larsen, and Allen Dunn (and Mary, too), for our moviegoing and film discussions over the years.

Thanks, finally, to my wife Nancy and son J.T., who enrich my life in so many ways. I'd like to dedicate this book to Nancy (again), as well as to my first film teachers, Ron Palosaari and the late John Mitchell, whose celebration of the rich and diverse possibilities of film art and culture continues to inspire me.

1 The Ending

Let's start at the end. The final shots of Charles Chaplin's *City Lights* (1931) constitute one of the most famous, memorable, and emotionally intricate endings of any movie in film history. In it Chaplin's iconic tramp character has just been released from prison, falsely accused of stealing money from a millionaire.[1] He has given that money to the blind flower girl (Virginia Cherrill), with whom he has fallen in love, to pay for an operation. Returning that love, she also believes the tramp to be a wealthy benefactor. While he has been in prison, the flower girl has had surgery and, her sight restored, has opened a prosperous florist shop, hoping that her beloved will return to her. When the bedraggled Charlie happens by her shop, he spies her through the store window, first looks puzzled and surprised, then smiles. She's amused at this tramp's reaction, yet comes to the door to offer him a flower and a coin as he shuffles away, afraid that she might recognise him, might see him as he really is. As he reaches a hand back to her into which she places the coin, she identifies the

The tramp, as downtrodden as he has ever been, looks despondent after a newspaper boy shoots peas at him in the final scene of *City Lights*

pitiable tramp as her benefactor. The framing tightens as shots of both characters respond to this shock of recognition. The last shot of the film, the tramp's response to the flower girl's acknowledgment that now she can see, is reproduced on the cover of this book.

This ending has entranced countless viewers around the globe since the film was released. It has also generated extensive commentary, perhaps none as memorable as James Agee's reflections in his 1950 essay, 'Comedy's Greatest Era':

At the end of City Lights the blind girl who has regained her sight, thanks to the tramp, sees him for the first time. She has imagined and anticipated him as princely, to say the least; and it has never seriously occurred to him that he is inadequate. She recognizes who he must be by his shy, confident, shining joy as he comes silently toward her. And he recognizes himself, for the first time, through the terrible changes in her face. The camera just exchanges a few quiet close-ups of the emotions which shift and intensify in each face. It is enough to shrivel the heart to see, and it is the greatest piece of acting and the highest moment in movies.[2]

Although Agee is, I believe, wrong in one detail – the flower girl first recognises the tramp not through her sight but through touch, by grasping his familiar hand – he's dead on target when he says that this ending 'shrivels the heart'.

Chaplin himself knew that this was a special moment in a special film. Discussing the final shot in a 1967 interview with Richard Meryman, Chaplin recalled,

I had had several takes and they were all overdone, overacted, overfelt. This time I was looking more at her. . . . It was the beautiful sensation of not acting, of standing outside of myself. The key was exactly right – slightly embarrassed, delighted about meeting her again – apologetic without getting emotional about it. He was watching and wondering what she was thinking and wondering without any effort. It's one of the purest inserts – I call them inserts, close-ups – that I've ever done. One of the purest.[3]

By the end of his career, Chaplin prized *City Lights*. In 1973, Peter Bogdanovich asked Chaplin, 'Which film of yours is your favorite? Can I ask you that? Or do you have no favorites?' Chaplin's reply: 'Oh, yes. I have. I like *City Lights*.'[4]

Examining the favourite film of one of the cinema's greatest figures may be reason enough to write about it. But there are other reasons, too. Commentators have long written about the protracted and difficult production of *City Lights*. As we shall see, a series of personal crises, industry shifts, and socio-cultural challenges combined to make this project a crucial one for Chaplin: the film-maker himself noted that shooting took such a long time because he kept wanting to make the film perfect. Furthermore, because Chaplin's surprisingly extensive production records are now available for scholars to examine at the Cineteca di Bologna, it is possible to trace with much more precision the production history of *City Lights*.

City Lights was a key transitional film for Chaplin – personally, aesthetically, and culturally. It was transitional because of the personal crises he endured just before and during the making of the film – his divorce from his second wife, Lita Grey, his separation from his sons of that marriage, Sydney and Charles Jr, and the death of his mother Hannah. It was transitional because of the aesthetic challenge of the film industry's shift to talkies, which took place while he was making *City Lights*: a master of pantomimic silent film comedy, Chaplin had to decide how he would respond to the challenge of the recorded soundtrack. It was transitional, finally, because he made *City Lights* while American culture itself was coping with the stock market crash, the end of the prosperity of the 1920s, and the beginnings of the downward economic spiral that resulted in the Great Depression.

Chaplin responded to these challenges with *City Lights*, and this book will look closely at the film, focusing on three concerns. I will first trace the production history of the film, as fully as is possible in a brief monograph, within the context of Chaplin's career. Second,

I will look closely at the film itself, probing how elements of narrative and cinematic style intertwine to communicate the film's key themes and to evoke its powerful and complex range of emotions, culminating in a detailed examination of the final scene that may help us appreciate more fully Chaplin's achievements. Finally, and more briefly, I will examine how audiences and commentators, in the original release and subsequently, have responded to Chaplin's 'Comedy Romance in Pantomime', closing with an assessment of the film's key place in Chaplin's filmmaking career.

2 Chaplin's Hollywood Roots

City Lights was indisputably a Charlie Chaplin film, made with a degree of creative control unusual in Hollywood, before or since. As the writer, director, star, composer, and producer of *City Lights*, Chaplin had collaborators, to be sure, but he could make films without interference from above to a degree that even noted directors like Vidor or Ford or Hawks or Capra could only dream of.

Chaplin's history in Hollywood explains how this came about. A successful London music-hall comedian, Chaplin twice toured North America with a British music-hall troupe, appearing in vaudeville theatres, where he drew the attention of people in the burgeoning movie industry. In December 1913 he began working for Mack Sennett at Keystone Studios. In his year at Keystone he is known to have appeared in thirty-five short comedies (plus the longer *Tillie's Punctured Romance*, 1914), assembled his now-famous tramp costume, began directing his films, earned $150/week, twice his music-hall salary, and increased this after three months to $175/week).[5]

By December 1914, the end of his year at Keystone, the tramp films were already popular, and companies were beginning to bid for Chaplin's services. His second contract with Essanay paid Chaplin $1,250 a week; there he made fourteen comedies in 1915 and 1916, and the nation experienced a case of what one commentator called 'Chaplinitis'.[6] The Mutual Film Corporation won his services in February 1916 by offering him $10,000 a week plus a $150,000 signing bonus to make twelve two-reelers. No small potatoes: according to a Consumer Price Index inflation calculator, Chaplin's $10,000/week salary in 1916 is equivalent to around $187,000 per week in 2006. His total pay from Mutual, bonus plus weekly salary ($670,000), would translate to over $12,500,000 in 2006 dollars.[7]

Through the years 1914–17, Chaplin was working for film
companies that paid him for his services and owned the films he
directed and in which he appeared. But Chaplin's shrewd path
toward independence took a new turn when he signed a contract in
June 1917 with the First National Exhibitors' Circuit. First National
was a newly formed entity composed of a group of theatre owners
who wished to buy films that they would, in turn, exhibit. Chaplin
agreed to make eight films for First National: he received a $75,000
signing bonus and $125,000 for each two-reel film he made to cover
his salary and production costs. First National paid for the prints and
advertising; they also received 30 per cent of the total rentals for their
distribution fees. Chaplin and First National divided the remaining
net profits equally.[8] A key if often overlooked feature of the
agreement was that after five years, the rights to his First National
films reverted to Chaplin. From this point on, Chaplin arranged
personally to own the rights to every subsequent film he made in the
United States, through to *Limelight* in 1952. That is a major reason
why we presently enjoy excellent prints of all the films from the First
National period on: Chaplin knew his films were valuable, and he
made sure they were well cared for.

Chaplin had two more tricks up his sleeve. The first was to
invest part of the fortune he had accrued by building his own studio.

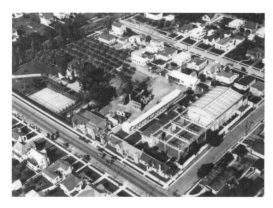

Aerial photograph of
Chaplin Studio,
1922–3, during the
shooting of A Woman
of Paris

In 1917 he purchased four acres of land in Hollywood, located south of Sunset Boulevard, east of La Brea Avenue, and north of Du Longpre Avenue, for $34,000. A house and tennis court already existed on the north of the property; to the south Chaplin built a studio that included two open stages, dressing rooms, offices, buildings for wardrobe, painting, and carpentry, a projection room, and even a film-developing laboratory. To reduce friction with his residential neighbours, he lined the western edge of his property, along La Brea, with building exteriors that looked like English cottages.[9] Nearly all the city we see in *City Lights* was created on this site.[10]

As Chaplin was fulfilling his First National contract, the movie business was consolidating. Early in 1919 rumours began flying that Paramount/Famous Players Lasky was planning to merge with First National, Chaplin's distributor, in part to combat spiralling star salaries. Led by Adolph Zukor, Paramount went on to become the first vertically integrated movie studio – a company that made films, then distributed them to theatres it owned. To counter this growing threat, on 15 January 1919, three of the most famous stars of the day – Chaplin, Douglas Fairbanks, and Mary Pickford – and the most widely known director, D. W. Griffith, joined to form United Artists, a company designed to market and distribute films that each of these artists produced independently. This final move made Chaplin an independent film-maker. All eight feature films he shot after fulfilling his First National contract, starting with *A Woman of Paris* in 1923 and stretching through to *Limelight* in 1952, were distributed through United Artists. Of them, the final shot of *City Lights*, the fourth film, and the opening shot of the fifth, *Modern Times* (1936), stand exactly in the middle.

3 Three Preceding Features

The first three United Artists films – *A Woman of Paris*, *The Gold Rush* (1925), and *The Circus* (1928) – established the groundwork and provided a backdrop for *City Lights*. All were feature-length films, with *Woman* running 7,577 feet, *Gold Rush* 8,555 feet, and *The Circus* a briefer 6,500 feet, each longer than Chaplin's longest film before these, *The Kid* (1920, at 5,250 feet). *City Lights* runs 8,093 feet.

A Woman of Paris was a departure for Chaplin, in part designed to show his versatility as a director and to enhance his reputation. Because tragedy maintains a higher cultural status than comedy, the successful comic sometimes hopes to play Hamlet. Witness Woody Allen's *Interiors* (1978), his Bergmanesque follow-up to *Annie Hall* (1977). *A Woman of Paris* is Chaplin's *Interiors*: a serious melodrama set in France, it was designed as a starring vehicle for Edna Purviance, who had played in most of Chaplin's comedies since the Essanay period as the object of the tramp's attentions. Chaplin himself appeared in the film only briefly, as an uncredited porter. Although the film did only moderately well at the box office, it did raise Chaplin's critical reputation and standing among the intelligentsia.

His status as an artist bolstered, Chaplin returned to tramp comedies with *The Gold Rush* and *The Circus*. Although his earliest and deepest roots were in the knockabout physical slapstick comedy of Keystone and the slightly more subtle comedy that featured the tramp's imaginative interaction with objects in his world, Chaplin was already experimenting with broadening the emotional range of his films through the introduction of pathos as early as *The Tramp* and *The Bank* in 1915, something he continued to hone in key scenes of films like *A Dog's Life*, *Shoulder Arms* (both 1918), and *The Kid*. *The Gold Rush*, a film highly praised in its day, artfully develops memorable comic scenes, like the Thanksgiving Day dinner of the tramp's shoe or the dance of the bread rolls on New Year's Eve – in the first, shoes become food, and in the second, food becomes shoes. Yet we also experience powerful moments of pathos in the film, as when, right after the bread roll dance, we discover that this has been a dream and that Georgia has jilted the tramp on New Year's Eve, letting him spend that most communal of holidays isolated and alone. The rapid shift of tone – here from delight and comedy to pathos – is something Chaplin expanded upon and perfected in *City Lights*. *The Circus* similarly exhibits this broad range of emotional appeal. The scenes of the tramp being chased by the police at the fun house and of his performance as a tight-rope walker – inhibited by monkeys crawling over and around him – provide a comic tone, but they are balanced by the scenes of unrequited love (when the tramp overhears that the circus rider's love is directed not at him but at Rex) and, ultimately, of human loneliness (when, in the final scene, the forlorn tramp, left behind, sits alone as everyone else in the circus rides off).

At the time he began to think about *City Lights*, Chaplin's public reputation was extremely high. Reviewing *Woman*, Robert Sherwood had hailed Chaplin as 'the first genius of the silent drama', while Stark Young called his creation, the tramp, 'one of the great clowns of all time'.[11] Moreover, by 1927 he had established through his comic films of the previous fifteen years a kind of 'aesthetic contract' with his enthusiastic audience. That is, Chaplin and his audience had developed an understanding that in exchange for buying a ticket, his fans could expect to experience a film that contained five elements: 1) a central comic persona, the tramp; 2) a romance between the tramp and the female lead; 3) inventive visual comedy; 4) integration of scenes that evoke pathos for the tramp or for another sympathetic character; and 5) a narrative involving two contrasting sets of values or moral perspectives. As *City Lights* began to percolate in his mind, Chaplin set out to perfect this formula. The experiences he went through in the year before he began shooting the film deepened and darkened his perspective and generated a greater urgency that his next film be a success.

4 Divorce and Tax Problems

In his autobiography Chaplin wrote that he had difficulty making
City Lights because 'I had worked myself into a neurotic state of
wanting perfection'.[12] That Chaplin suffered 'neurotic' strain may be
no surprise: just before and during the making of *City Light*s he was
confronted by a number of financial, emotional, and aesthetic
challenges. The first two hit Chaplin hard in January 1927 and
dogged him throughout the year and beyond. The first was the
divorce complaint that his second wife, Lita Grey Chaplin, levied
against him. The couple had married in 1924, and they had two
children together: Sydney, born in 1925, and Charles Jr, born early in
1926. Estranged in part because of Chaplin's absorption in his work,
Lita had left him, taking their sons with her, in late November 1926.
Chaplin was about three-quarters through the shooting of *The Circus*
but, remembering his experience with *The Kid* during his first divorce
– when he had to flee the state with the film stock to continue editing
the film – and worrying that his assets would be frozen, Chaplin
suspended production on 5 December and had his film footage boxed
up. Lita's uncle, lawyer Edwin McMurray, moved to Los Angeles
from San Francisco, assembled a legal team, and set to work. On 10
January 1927, the lawyers filed a long divorce complaint that charged
Chaplin with 'cruel and inhuman' treatment of Lita and claimed that
he indulged in sexual practices 'too revolting, indecent and immoral
to set forth in detail'.[13] Chaplin immediately responded by taking a
train to New York and having the footage of *The Circus* sent east
with him.[14] The press, particularly in Los Angeles, had a field day:
within a couple of days newsboys were selling cheap copies of the
complaint on the city streets. A week later, on 17 January, Judge
Walter Guerin ordered Chaplin's property to be placed in the hands

of a receiver and directed Chaplin to pay living expenses to Lita and their sons until the case was settled.[15]

As Chaplin travelled to New York, insult followed injury: the federal government claimed that he owed back taxes as far back as 1918. These twin blows traumatised Chaplin, so much so that, according to his doctor, he suffered a nervous breakdown after his arrival in New York. News only got worse over the next two weeks: a government spokesman announced on the 22nd that Chaplin owed $1.13 million of back taxes on his personal income, and by 28 January, federal officials had placed liens on his United Artists assets until he could put up funds to guarantee payment.[16] Whatever his medical condition may have been, he clearly suffered deep distress. Chaplin later told his associate Harry Crocker – who played the tight-rope walker Rex in *The Circus* and helped with the screenplays of that film and *City Lights* – that while in New York, he often stayed in his lawyer Nathan Burkan's apartment, 'expecting to be arrested at any moment'.[17]

Several weeks after the news broke, Chaplin's brother Syd wrote him a note of advice and encouragement. It opened, 'Because I have not written you certainly is not that I lack sympathy – you are continually in my thoughts. I hate to imagine how you must have felt when you were on that train, alone, and the news broke. It was like a bomb-shell to me.' Often an adviser to his brother about business, he added later in the letter, 'I certainly would not pay her a million nor for that matter make any settlement until the government suit was out of the way. Certainly if worse comes to worse the government will take so much there will be nothing left for her anyway.' He then closed the letter urging optimism:

Do not get too despondent, Charlie. Remember there is more in life than great wealth – as long as you know you are comfortably fixed for the future and your health is good, it should help to maintain a philosophical attitude toward your troubles. When I am feeling sort of worried, myself, I always think of the great joy, happiness and elated feeling I had when I signed on the dotted line for Fred Karno – just think the great sum of three pounds a week – why I ran all the way to Kennington Road to send you the glad news. So it seems afterall, that happiness is a matter of comparison and dependent upon our own viewpoint or way of thinking. So CHEER UP OLD KID.[18]

This advice takes on interesting significance – indeed, submerged autobiographical resonance – when we think of the tramp's attempts in *City Lights* to cheer up the suicidal millionaire, whose wife has just left him.

Syd had reason to worry about Charlie. The tax dispute and the divorce negotiations persisted, and Chaplin remained in New York until August, when his lawyers had nearly settled the divorce case. On 19 August, shortly before the case was about to go before the judge for a decision, the lawyers reached a settlement. Lita was awarded child custody, and Chaplin agreed to pay her $625,000 and to set up $100,000 trust funds for each of his sons in the following schedule: Chaplin paid her $375,000 at the time of settlement, $100,000 in each of the next two years, and the remaining $50,000 in 1930. He also agreed to some other expenses, including outstanding debts accrued by Lita before their separation, child-support payments until the trust funds were set up in 1930, and part of the receivership fees. *Variety* reported that these direct costs added up to around $950,000 but that once all expenses were calculated, including significant legal fees and the cost of closing down production on *The Circus*, the divorce cost Chaplin closer to $2 million.[19] The Interlocutory Judgment of Divorce was completed on 23 August, with the divorce to become official on that same day the following year.[20]

The tax problem, however, lingered. The uncertainty of its outcome placed enough additional financial pressure on Chaplin to finish *The Circus* and start another project, but the eventual settlement made that pressure even more concrete. In February 1928 the *New York Times* reported that the Bureau of Internal Revenue had lifted the liens on Chaplin's bank accounts in January because he had paid the $1.67 million he owed in back taxes: $1,073,000 in personal income taxes and the rest in corporate taxes from the Charles Chaplin Film Corporation.[21] The divorce and tax problems of 1927–8 thus cost the film-maker well over $3.5 million. Furthermore, the distress he felt throughout the long period the cases remained unsettled, not knowing what effect the legal and financial problems would have on his life and career, surely contributed to the 'neurotic state' he felt while making *City Lights*.

5 Hannah

About a week after the divorce case was settled, Sydney Chaplin wrote to Charlie from London, expressing how glad he was that the divorce was settled out of court, even though it cost him a 'tremendous sum'. Turning to the future, Syd expressed confidence that Chaplin would return to more financial stability when he finished *The Circus* and indicated his 'hope you will be able to take up the thread of the story and continue as enthusiastic as you were when you started'.[22] Chaplin heeded Syd's advice: he returned to California in August, resumed production on *The Circus* on 5 September, finished cutting on 17 November, and premiered the film first at the Strand Theater in New York on 6 January 1928, and then three weeks later at Grauman's Chinese Theater in Hollywood. Uncharacteristically – but understandably, given the financial pressures – Chaplin took no extended break between pictures. Alf Reeves, long-time Chaplin studio business manager, wrote to Syd on 9 December that Charlie probably wouldn't attend the New York premiere: 'If he sticks to his present resolve, he will start another picture shortly here.'[23] And that's what happened: the studio's production report for the week ending 31 December 1927 contains the first reference to his new film: 'Mr Chaplin talking over material for next picture.' Weekly reports continued through the week ending 12 May 1928, usually indicating that Chaplin was working on the story for the next film, although the report on this date was slightly different: for the first time, the new project's working title was specified – *City Lights*.[24]

Work on the story continued throughout the summer, and Australian artist Henry Clive was assigned to provide sketches for sets. Under the supervision of Charles D. ('Danny') Hall, who had worked with Chaplin as Art Director since the First National period,

CHARLES CHAPLIN FILM CORPORATION		**DAILY** PRODUCTION REPORT		NUMBER OF DAYS ON PICTURE INCLUDING TO-DAY		
				IDLE	WORK	TOTAL

DIRECTOR	CHARLIE CHAPLIN		DATE	May 12,	192 8
CAMERAMAN	Roland Totheroh		PICTURE NO.	Comedy #3, U.A.C.	
WORKING TITLE	"City Lights"		NUMBER OF REELS	6	

CAST	RATE	SCENES PLAYED IN	PETTY CASH EXPENDITURES	
			ARTICLE	AMOUNT
			BALANCE ON HAND	
Charlie Chaplin				
Henry Bergman				
Harry Crocker				
Merna Kennedy				
			STILLS TAKEN TO-DAY	
			NUMBER BROUGHT FORWARD	
			TOTAL STILLS TO DATE	

SCENES TAKEN TODAY						FILM USED		STARTED WORK	
SCENE NO.	FEET	SCENE NO.	FEET	SCENE NO.	FEET	FOOTAGE		A. M.	P. M.
	FORWARD		FORWARD			TODAY			
						BAL. FORWD.			
						TOTAL TO DATE			
						MEMO.			

Mr. Chaplin and staff working on story for next picture. Tests being taken for lights and make-up.

TOTAL	TOTAL	GRAND TOT.					
AUTO USED		STARTED TIME A.M. / P.M.	FINISHED TIME A.M. / P.M.	*Fair*		WEATHER { FAIR / CLOUDY / RAIN	
				O.K. *Della R Steele*			CLERK

This weekly production report for 12 May 1928 was the first for which the working title is *City Lights*. Note the signature of Della R. Steele, Chaplin's continuity reporter, who prepared the reports

some set construction even began in early August. Then another emotional crisis jolted Charlie: his mother, Hannah, died on 28 August 1928.

Chaplin's relationship with his mother was complex. Both his parents were music-hall singers, but Chaplin's father separated from Hannah within a year of Chaplin's birth in 1889, eventually dying in 1901, his health seriously undermined by alcoholism. When Hannah's voice faltered, she initially tried to support her sons as a seamstress with erratic help from her former husband. However, beginning in 1895, when Chaplin was only six, Hannah began suffering mental problems and was in and out of institutions like the Cane Hill Asylum, while her sons spent time – sometimes alone, sometimes together – in places like the Hanwell Institute for Orphans and Destitute Children or occasionally with relatives. Both

Sydney and Charlie cut their educations short and started working early – Charlie with a clog-dancing group called the Eight Lancashire Lads late in 1898 – and they eventually began earning enough to help care for their mother when periods of remission permitted her to leave Cane Hill. In early March 1905, when the fifteen-year-old Charlie was on tour with a play called *Sherlock Holmes*, Hannah suffered another relapse, returned to Cane Hill, and never recovered. The pain of being unable to help his mother – he couldn't even visit her until he finished his tour in late April – left an indelible stamp on Charlie.[25]

Syd and Charlie's growing financial security enabled them eventually to afford private care for their mother, and in March 1921 – following his traumatic first divorce and the creative energies he expended on *The Kid* – Charlie arranged for Hannah to come to California. There she was cared for by Mr and Mrs William Carey, who lived in North Hollywood. Yet Chaplin could not bring himself to visit her often, because her condition would frequently leave him despondent and unable to work. In 1998 Jeffrey Vance interviewed Wyn Ritchie Evans, whose mother, Winifred, worked at times as a costumer at the Chaplin studio and who sometimes visited Hannah with her mother. Evans recalled that 'Charlie didn't want anyone to know about his mother for fear of headlines like "Charlie Chaplin's Insane Mother."' She remembered Hannah as 'brilliant' and capable of clever imitations at times but also recalled occasions when her behaviour became uncontrolled and erratic.[26]

In mid-August 1928 Hannah, who had been resting for several weeks in Encinitas with the Careys, began having complications from a gall-bladder condition and was taken by ambulance to the Physicians and Surgeons Hospital in Glendale. Alf Reeves wrote to Syd on the 27th that Chaplin had been visiting her every day and added: 'At the time of writing her condition seems very serious, and they are hoping for the best. However, it must be said things look rather bad at this time, as I have heard today she has had a setback.'[27] The next day Charlie telegrammed Syd, 'Our dear mother passed away peacefully midday. Love, Charlie.' An Episcopal funeral service was held at the Hollywood Cemetery on 30 August, a bright, sunny day, with Charlie the only family member in attendance, along with fewer than twenty friends. One who attended noted that when the casket was being lowered into the ground, a 'large black-and-yellow butterfly fluttered from the blue to poise for a moment upon the flowers, then soared aloft until its erratic flight was lost to sight. It produced a breathtaking finale to the service.'[28] Alf Reeves wrote to Sydney on 31 August that despite the fact that 'Charlie did not wish any ostentation or display at the funeral', there was a 'beautiful blanket of roses on the casket "From Charles and Syd," and there were many floral emblems', along with messages of condolence.[29]

In his autobiography Chaplin describes how, sitting at his mother's deathbed and thinking about her life of struggle, he wept. His final reference to his mother follows later on the same page: 'In spite of the squalor in which we were forced to live, she had kept Sydney and me off the streets and made us feel we were not the ordinary product of poverty, but unique and distinguished' (*MA*,

Chaplin's telegram to his brother Syd on the day that his mother died

p. 298). Friends indicated that Chaplin was devastated by his mother's death. Given that the film script was still far from complete when Hannah passed away, Jeffrey Vance offers a valuable insight when he suggests that 'it is perhaps no coincidence that in his new film his character rescued a disabled woman and caused her to be cured of her affliction' (p. 195). Without a doubt the personal loss contributed to the emotional complexity and power of *City Lights*.

6 The Challenge of the Talkies

As if the divorce, tax problems, and Hannah's death were not enough, a serious aesthetic challenge arose as Chaplin began *City Lights*: the emergence of the talkies. As a film-maker whose reputation rested on his brilliance as a pantomimic performer and director in silent film comedies, Chaplin was confronted with a serious dilemma when the film industry enthusiastically added recorded sound, including dialogue, to the visual aesthetics of American movies. And that challenge first faced Chaplin squarely as he contemplated and made *City Lights*.

A time-line might help here. Warner Bros.' *Don Juan*, using the Vitaphone sound system to provide recorded musical accompaniment, premiered in August 1926, when Chaplin was midway through the shooting schedule of *The Circus*. Warners' second Vitaphone feature, *The Better 'Ole*, a slapstick silent comedy with synchronised score, starred none other than Syd Chaplin and opened on 7 October 1926, about two months before Charlie suspended production on *The Circus* because of marital discord. *The Jazz Singer*, the first important feature film that included some scenes with synchronised dialogue, premiered one day short of a year later, on 6 October 1927, a little more than a month before Chaplin finished cutting *The Circus* after the divorce settlement. However, at this time few theatres were wired for sound. That transition happened over the next two years: by the October 1929 stock market crash, Donald Crafton notes, 'out-of-the-way theaters and those servicing poor neighborhoods were the only ones still waiting for amplification. The transformation of American movie houses from almost all silent to almost all sound therefore took about a year and a half.'[30] By the month of the crash, Chaplin was still in the early stages of *City Lights*, shooting and editing the café sequence with the millionaire and the tramp. The musical *Broadway*

Melody was a current hit, and even Chaplin's United Artists' partners, Douglas Fairbanks and Mary Pickford, premiered their first talkie, *Taming of the Shrew*, at the end of October 1929. As Chaplin moved more deeply into the shooting schedule of *City Lights*, then, the movie industry was rapidly abandoning silent cinema and embracing the talkies.

How did Chaplin respond to this change? About six months after the release of *The Jazz Singer*, Chaplin was willing to try out his voice with the public on a radio broadcast. On 29 March 1928, when Chaplin was still in the very early story stages of *City Lights*, the NBC Radio Network broadcast the *Dodge Brothers Hour* from New York and from Douglas Fairbanks's studio bungalow in Hollywood to fifty-five NBC affiliates and a number of movie theatres in larger US cities. Paul Whiteman and his band played from the New York studio of WJZ, and when the programme linked to Hollywood, Douglas Fairbanks talked on 'Keeping Fit', Norma Talmadge discussed Hollywood fashions, D. W. Griffith spoke on 'Love', Chaplin told 'characteristic stories', and John Barrymore delivered a *Hamlet* soliloquy.[31]

The experience did little to encourage Chaplin to dive into the talkies. A *Variety* reporter who spoke to Chaplin after the broadcast wrote 'that he nearly died while doing it, through mike fright, and was worried as to how he did'. The same article discussed the reactions of movie theatre audiences to hearing their movie idols speak. A Boston audience started 'the razz' to get back to the scheduled movie, and a Baltimore theatre owner probably stated the majority opinion of owners and audiences, when he said they should not have to listen to entertainers 'whose talents are essentially visual'.[32] If part of Chaplin's reason for participating in the event was to try out his voice with audiences before deciding whether his next film would be a talkie, the experience could hardly have encouraged him.

Yet Chaplin seems not to have decided definitively about dialogue until sometime early in 1929. In July 1928, when he was still working on the story of *City Lights*, Chaplin told reporters that he was not yet certain whether the film would have sound effects, music, or dialogue.[33] In January 1929 Alf Reeves wrote to Syd Chaplin that filming had begun, but the production was 'not yet much advanced', adding that Charlie 'fully intends to make one version with sound' and also a 'universal picture for those countries where they have not facilities for the new inventions'.[34]

By May 1929, however, he had cast his lot as an aesthetic traditionalist – at least regarding dialogue in films. When asked his opinion of talkies, Chaplin replied, 'You can tell 'em I loathe them. . . . They are spoiling the oldest art in the world, the art of pantomime.'[35] From that point on until the release of *City Lights* in January 1931, Chaplin regularly denounced the talkies and celebrated the art of pantomime that was so central to his success and the achievements of films in the silent era.

It was a calculated risk. As the production of *City Lights* progressed, talkies came almost completely to dominate the American movie industry. Yet Chaplin believed that refusing dialogue in his movies would permit him to maintain his huge non-English-language following more easily than if he capitulated to talkies. He worried, too, that his British accent would have seemed strange and inappropriate to some who knew the tramp only as a silent film character. In addition, in the late 1920s many intellectuals – who often celebrated Chaplin and whose favour Chaplin enjoyed – took a similar position, defending the purity of silent film art in the face of the scratchy chatter and static visual style of much early sound cinema. So several compelling reasons persuaded Chaplin to make a non-dialogue film.

One must emphasise, however, that Chaplin did not entirely reject the recorded soundtrack. As early as 28 April 1929 Alf Reeves wrote to Sydney Chaplin that he was working on a very promising sequence – what turned out to be the opening statue scene – and added that he was shooting it 'as usual but of course sound effects, if required, can be added afterwards'.[36] Ultimately, Chaplin decided on a compromise solution to the challenge of sound: he would include a musical score with some sound effects but entirely refuse spoken language. As we shall see, that decision and Chaplin's engagement in composing the film's score contributed significantly to the overall final effect of *City Lights*.

Taken together, his divorce from Lita Grey Chaplin, his tax problems, the death of his mother, and the emergence of the talkies posed serious challenges to Chaplin as he faced shooting his next film after *The Circus*. How, given this context, was Chaplin able to struggle through the production and emerge with his masterpiece on the other side?

7 Refining a Story

Film production in Hollywood may be conveniently divided into three stages: pre-production, production, and post-production. Pre-production includes arranging the financing, preparing a script, and planning sets and costumes. Production comprises the actual shooting of the film. Post-production involves editing the film and preparing the soundtrack, including the musical score, to ready the film for general release.

In part because he owned his own studio and paid for his own productions, Chaplin intertwined these three stages in a manner atypical in Hollywood. For example, because he financed his own films, Chaplin didn't go through the same budgeting process that a studio like MGM or Warner Bros. would follow in pre-production before a film was officially approved for shooting. Chaplin's desires constituted the financial green light. Second, as was his practice on previous silent film comedies, on *City Lights* Chaplin started shooting the film with a general story but without a tightly prepared shooting script, preferring instead to refine the story during production: pre-production thus bled into the shooting stage of the film. Finally, Chaplin usually concentrated on one scene at a time and supervised preliminary editing of these individual scenes during the shooting stage of the film: post-production thus intruded sharply into shooting, too. After the initial editing of some *City Lights* scenes, like the first meeting of the tramp and the flower girl, Chaplin would, if necessary, return to that set for retakes – in this case, several times – and then further refine the editing. That's one reason why the final film could be edited and prepared relatively quickly after the shooting stage was completed: shooting the last footage on 30 October 1930, Chaplin had the film, including the recorded musical score that he co-wrote with Arthur Johnston after

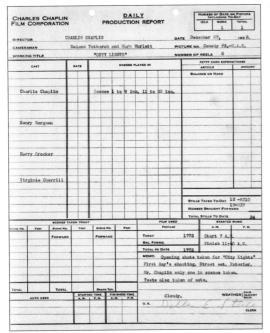

This is the first daily production report (DPR), taken on the initial day of shooting *City Lights*. None of the footage shot on this day was used in the film

shooting ended, ready for a 19 January 1931 preview at the Tower Theater in Los Angeles.[37]

The production reports and other production records housed in the Cineteca di Bologna enable one to tell the story of the making of *City Lights*. The first DPR was prepared on the first day of shooting: 27 December 1928. Thereafter, the DPRs continued, usually from Monday to Saturday each week, through to 6 February 1931, the day *City Lights* premiered at the Cohan Theater in Manhattan. These DPRs, supplemented by many other production documents – including story ideas, continuity lists, script versions, a master list of all the takes for the film, cutting continuity lists, and so on – allow us to reconstruct fairly precisely the production history of the movie.[38]

Chaplin's first challenge was coming up with a story. Typically for him, once he began making feature films, this took a long time.

Partly because of the financial pressures discussed above, he began thinking about the story during the last week of 1927, even before *The Circus* was released, and nearly all the WPRs throughout 1928 say something like 'Mr Chaplin and staff working on story' or, less often, 'Mr Chaplin and Mr Crocker working on story'. Harry Crocker, who was regularly involved in Chaplin's story conferences on both *The Circus* and *City Lights*, wrote about those experiences in his unpublished biography of Chaplin. Crocker tells us that the story conferences took place in a bungalow in the quiet northeast corner of Chaplin's studio grounds. These conferences usually included Chaplin's private secretary Carlyle Robinson, Crocker, Henry Bergman, and perhaps one or two others. 'There are periods

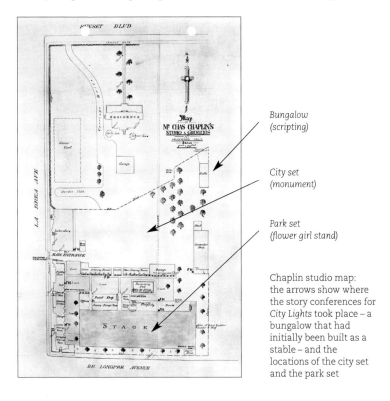

Bungalow
(scripting)

City set
(monument)

Park set
(flower girl stand)

Chaplin studio map: the arrows show where the story conferences for *City Lights* took place – a bungalow that had initially been built as a stable – and the locations of the city set and the park set

An early version of the story starts with a dream sequence set in Venice. The tramp, 'resplendent in uniform', gives a diamond necklace to a beautiful woman. The scene would end with the tramp on a park bench, awakened by a licking dog. Chaplin shot a screen test but never shot the scene. Even in later versions of the story, the flower girl refers to the tramp as 'the Duke'.

in the creation of his stories', Crocker wrote, 'when Charlie deliberately invited his workmen to "yes" him, to agree with him, to enthuse with him. These come in the preliminary stages when he is groping for ideas. There is always a time for critical analysis of material. During the evolution of ideas there should be no effort to analyze, to criticize.' Crocker also quotes Chaplin's admission: 'I would love to work methodically, but I can't do it.'[39] In this sense Chaplin's intuitive method of story development – one that continued into the shooting stage of the film – was quite unlike, say, the working methods of a Hitchcock, who methodically analysed his way through story construction and storyboarding so that, as he put it, the most creative work of filmmaking was finished before he even started shooting.

Very early on in the story development, Chaplin established several concepts crucial to the final film: 1) having a blind flower girl and a millionaire as two key characters interacting with the tramp; 2) having the blind girl fall in love with the tramp, whom she would believe to be rich (she calls him 'the Duke' in many of the story notes); 3) having the millionaire befriend the tramp when drunk and reject him when sober; and 4) ending the film by having the flower girl, her sight restored, meet and recognise the tramp. However, it took a long time to pare down countless other story ideas to the final simplicity, clarity, and power of the finished film.

A look at some story notes illustrates how the story changed. Take, for example, this list of scenes titled 'Episodes of Continuity'. Undated, it was probably prepared sometime during the 1928 story conferences before shooting began. Of the fifteen scenes listed, at least six of them never appear (1, 2, 4, 10, 12, and 13), and the continuity had not yet included the monument scene, the nude statue scene, the boxing scenes, the street-cleaner scenes, and so on. Note, too, that Chaplin had not yet established that the flower girl's world and the millionaire's world would be separate: scenes 10, 12, and 13 suggest

Episodes of Continuity.

1. The Princess and the officer.

2. The introduction of Charlie in tramp character with the dog.

3. The Tramp's meeting with the blind flower girl.

4. The fight between the cabman and the Tramp.

5. The millionaire drunkard's interest in the Tramp.

6. The relationship of the millionaire with the Tramp while drunk and the relationship of the millionaire with the Tramp when sober.

7. The entrance of the Tramp into the millionaire's home.

8. The exit of the Tramp from the millionaire's home.

9. The Tramp's attitude toward the blind flower girl.

10. The meeting of the millionaire with the blind flower girl and the Tramp when the millionaire is drunk.

11. The disappearance of the Tramp.

12. The meeting of the millionaire while sober with the blind flower girl.

13. The return of the blind flower girl with regained eyesight and the pursuit of the millionaire for her hand in marriage.

14. The blind flower girl's dream of the return of her ideal.

15. The return of the Tramp and the ignorance as to his identity by the flower girl and the Tramp's realization that he should conceal his identity and face the world alone.

This page contains a list of scenes from the early story development of *City Lights* that the two characters would interact and that the millionaire would even pursue the flower girl.

Considerable uncertainty about the story continued through much of 1929. For example, one page of story notes headed 'Continuity of Story as of June 6, 1929' attempted to set out the order of scenes in the early part of the story, and I have added bold letters to those scenes that did eventually make it into the early part of the finished film:

Dream – Awakening – Wandering – **Statue** – City busy – Albert – **Art Store** – Chip – **Girl** – Fade out – Fade In – Banana – 6 o'clock – People Going Home – Helping girl across street – **Girl at home** – **Predicament of Girl** – **Charlie meets drunk** – **Home of Drunk** – **Cafe** – **Meets girl Again**.[40]

Story notes up to that time suggested that the film would start with a dream sequence. In one version a beautiful and wealthy woman in an apartment overlooking a park orders her 'Hindu servant' to fetch a tramp she sees from her window. She would kiss and offer the tramp food, after which he would be awakened from his dream by a dog licking him, then chased by a policeman, and forced to wander around the city. The statue dedication scene would follow. The first

The 'chip' scene was completed but never used in City Lights

few days of shooting around New Year's Day 1929, although not used in the final film, were apparently related to the 'Wandering' part of the story, and the dream sequence was never shot. The 'chip' incident in the 6 June continuity that follows the art store episode refers to a scene, shot but never used in the film, of the tramp trying to dislodge a chip of wood from a pavement grate in front of a store display window.[41] Although the eventual order of the opening scenes was beginning to take shape, the story was still not sharply focused as of June 1929.

In addition, many details that would eventually be central to the film's success were not yet worked out, even when the broad story conceptions were. One undated fourteen-page story summary, probably from 1928, describes the final scene in which the flower girl recognises the tramp, yet in quite different details. According to the story summary, the film will end like this:

As she places the flower in his buttonhole she instinctively recognizes the little man and her eyes become filled as her quivering lips speak: 'The Duke.' He gazes at her as the little sister starts the phonograph record 'Bright Eyes,' and the record whirls out into the finish.[42]

At least four key details here differ from the finished film: the flower girl's sister gets cut from the story, the final song is changed, the flower girl first recognises the tramp not by his coat but by touching his hand, and the final shot is not of a whirling record but a close-up of the tramp's face. Chaplin was a prolific brain-stormer, and part of his working method was gradually to discard details and sharpen focus throughout the production.

Story refinements thus continued through the entire shooting stage. Once Chaplin began to develop a positive shooting momentum in the autumn of 1929, the DPRs suggest that he concentrated on one scene at a time: refining the script, shooting, and then editing it. Usually when Chaplin finished shooting a scene that he was relatively satisfied with, he stopped shooting and edited for several days. At the same time he would plan more precisely the story details of a new scene, and his crew would prepare the sets for it. A good example is a three-page story note headed 'Story as of Feb. 28, 1930'. The DPRs show that Chaplin and his staff were working on scripting a new sequence from 14 February on. The 28 February story notes summarise the development of the final scenes of the film, from the time the flower girl falls ill until the mutual recognition in the film's final scene. Although some details are still different, much of the description from the scene in which Charlie gets money from the millionaire to use for the blind girl's operation through to the conclusion is very similar to the realisation in the final film. Note how this description of the final shots is much closer to the finished film compared to the previous example:

Slowly the Tramp comes to her and as he stretches his hand out for the flower, she grips his wrist and pulls him closer. A strangeness takes hold of her and there is recognition. She seems dazed. He bows his head in acknowledgment and a great emotion rises in the girl; a thousand things run through her mind and then she smiles through her tears as the scene ends.[43]

Ultimately, of course, the finished film depended as much on such elements as performance, cinematography, editing, and the soundtrack as it did on the script. Nevertheless, the story slowly became tightened, refined, and sharpened from the beginnings in late 1928 until October 1930, when the shooting finally ended.

8 The Production Record in Perspective

City Lights has long had the reputation of being an extremely troubled production, and material from the Chaplin Archives in some ways supports this, particularly until December 1929. It was certainly a *long* production. The four-page 'Production Record: *City Lights*' indicates, for example, that the shooting began on 27 December 1928 and ended on 30 November 1930: 673 days. Eliminate around 100 days of Sundays and holidays during that period, and over 570 days remain – an enormous span considering that a typical Hollywood feature shooting schedule ran four to eight weeks. Another telling detail from the same document: of the 683 total days worked from the start of story preparation through the completion of the editing and scoring, shooting occurred on only 179 of those days, while 504 days were listed on the form as 'idle'. Finally, the document notes that Chaplin shot 314,256 feet of film. The completed film ran 8,093 feet, making a shooting ratio of between 38 and 39 feet shot for each foot that made it into the final film. One given to understatement might say that Chaplin exercised considerable care and devoted significant effort to making the film.

However, because the same Production Record defines 'idle' days as 'preparation of story, rehearsing, cutting, etc.', it's evident that Chaplin was often working on those 'idle' days. In addition, neither the ratio of shooting days to 'idle' days nor the shooting ratio itself was extreme for Chaplin, a notorious perfectionist once he gained control of his films. Take a look at the chart (overleaf), which compares the production schedules and shooting ratios of four Chaplin feature comedies.

Note that *The Circus* used nearly as many shooting days as *City Lights*, even though the finished film was about 20 per cent shorter. Note, too, that although Chaplin's shooting ratio on *City Lights* was

Film	Shooting days	'Idle' days	Total days	Shooting ratio
The Circus	170	467	637	32:1
City Lights	179	504	683	39:1
Modern Times	147	263	410	26:1
The Great Dictator	168	391	559	38:1

higher than on *The Circus* and *Modern Times*, it was just about the same on *The Great Dictator*.[44]

In fact, production records suggest that although Chaplin admittedly had a great deal of difficulty starting the film, once the shooting entered its central phase, the production ran relatively smoothly, if painstakingly, with the exception of one or two dilemmas that Chaplin had difficulty solving. Evidence even suggests that Chaplin was not always in a 'neurotic state of perfection' when he was making the film but that he sometimes worked with efficiency and even considerable pleasure. I'd like to develop this perspective on the production of *City Lights* in the next two sections by outlining the rhythm of the shooting schedule and identifying the chief problem points that Chaplin faced as he shot the film.

9 A Troubled Production: To November 1929

Driven by financial pressures, besieged by the emotional traumas of divorce and, later, the death of his mother, and indecisive about how to respond to the challenge of sound films, Chaplin initially had a hard time making progress on *City Lights*. That may seem surprising given that the final film, in Alistair Cooke's fine description, flows 'like water over pebbles, smooth and simple for all to see'.[45] Production records help us pinpoint the difficulties and pressure points in the production. They also permit us to note the rhythm of the production – what went well and what did not, what was smooth and what was rocky. Let's look first at roughly the first half of the production period.

Chaplin began planning the story for *City Lights* just after Christmas Day, 1927, before releasing *The Circus*, shooting his first footage about a year later. The production reports, however, suggest that Chaplin hoped to begin shooting even earlier: the WPR of 5 May 1928 optimistically indicated 'costumes being fitted and ordered. Make-up tests being taken – preparing to start work,' and for the first time, the next week's report indicated that the new production would be called *City Lights* and that further tests were being taken 'for lights and makeup'. Things slowed down during June and July, with work continuing on the script and Henry Clive preparing sketches for the sets. Although Hannah Chaplin's deteriorating medical condition, culminating in her death on 28 August, slowed down Chaplin from mid-August on, during that month his collaborator C. D. 'Danny' Hall began supervising set construction, while Mike Marlett was hired to assist cinematographer Rollie Totheroh, Chaplin's regular cameraman since the mid-1910s. Between the start of August and the middle of October, Hall supervised the building of the city in *City Lights*. Although we'll come back to the set design below, note that the principal exterior sets were the 'park set' where the flower girl's

Aerial shot of Chaplin studio during the middle 1930s. After completing *City Lights*, Chaplin enclosed the open stage where the park set was built. The star shows the approximate location of the flower stand. The triangle shows the approximate location of the city set monument. Note that three of the four blocks of storefronts (numbered 1–3) from the *City Lights* city set are still standing. The fourth was across the street to the left of the upper block, forming a square of four blocks. The small arrow points toward the approximate place where the flower girl hands the tramp the rose at the end of the film.

stand is located, built on the open stage on the southwest corner of the studio, and the 'city set' that includes the 'Peace and Prosperity' monument and most of the store fronts we see in the film. That set was built in the open lot, just north of the garage and men's dressing rooms, west and south of the bungalow where Chaplin worked on the script. The 'T' design concealed the finite nature of the city set.

Although progress on the script was slow, Virginia Cherrill signed a contract on 16 October to appear in the film as the blind flower girl; her first day of work was 5 November.[46] Merna Kennedy's name had been listed as a member of the cast on the production reports during October – she had played the romantic female lead in *The Circus* – but her name was dropped thereafter, and Cherrill's appeared first on the 11 November DPR, where it remained throughout the production, save for a brief period a year after she first arrived.

Work on the script and sets continued through Christmas, and

Chaplin finally decided to start shooting *something* on 27 December. A look at the shooting notations of the first day shows that he was shooting the tramp wandering in the city in the vicinity of the park and flower girl's stand. He continued shooting footage of this scene, which was originally to have appeared after the tramp awakened from his dream, through to 9 January, although he didn't even keep track of the shot numbers for the last two days, and not a single foot of what was shot made it into *City Lights*. Stymied, Chaplin stopped

"CITY LIGHTS"

Opening Shots - December 27, 1928.

Thursday - 7 A.M.

Scene 1. - Longshot - Exterior street showing full cast side with background of tall buildings. C.C. comes from left of camera on street side nearest camera after fade in. He walks slowly to the corner where he stands and yawns. He carries his cane in his left hand and his right hand is plunged in his trouser pocket. His coat collar is turned up. He then starts across the street away from the camera, strolling slowly. He favors the curb. About three-quarter way in the block, fades out.
(Mr. Chaplin's costume - Derby hat, Scott Bros, American, Cuffs with flat buttons, grey trousers, checked vest, old greenish coat.)
O.K.-78

Scene 2. - Retake. In this shot C.C. lingers longer at corner and faces full to camera than starts his walk. As he crosses the street, the street lights go out.
O.K.-89

Scene 3. - Retake. This scene was interrupted when electricity went off.
O.K.-29

Scene 4. - Retake. In this shot, C.C. stands on corner with right profile to camera and as he crosses street after lights go out, he lingers and then starts walk.
O.K.-120

Scene 5. - Retake. Note: The sun is now coming up.
O.K.-110

Scene 6. - Retake. Note: The sun is higher.
O.K.-105

Scene 7. - Retake. Note: In this shot the corner lamps are turned around parallel.
O.K.-105

Scene 8. - Corner lights are not used in this shot. Sun is now high.
N.G.-15

Scene 9. - In this shot C.C. stands longer on the corner and it is a sort of test for sound.
O.K.-115

Scene 10.- A test of the set without C.C.

Scene 11.- Retake. It is now 10:30 A.M. and there is a diffused light, due to cloudiness.
O.K.-85

Scene 12.- Retake.
O.K.-87

Scene 13. - Retake.
O.K.-70

Scene 14.- Retake.
O.K.-76

Scene 15.- Retake. 11 A.M. Cloudy.
O.K.-78

1.

This is the first page of shooting notations for *City Lights* – 27 December 1928. Chaplin eventually took over 4500 shots (called 'scenes' in the notations) while making the film

shooting, went with Crocker and Clive to William Randolph Hearst's
San Simeon mansion, worked on the script for a few days, and after
nearly three weeks had passed, began shooting on 28 January the
initial meeting at the flower girl's stand.[47] He continued shooting this
scene with the tramp and the flower girl until 14 February, often with
over twenty extras on the set, amassing 236 takes over the period.
Things clearly weren't working well: not a foot of that material made
it into the final cut. Chaplin then stopped shooting for nearly a week,
trying to decide how to proceed. When he resumed, on 20 February,
the DPR noted that Chaplin was 'changing action of sequence at the
Flower Stand', and he shot another twenty-odd takes over the next
two days, none of which was used either.

Chaplin and journalist
Egon Erwin Kisch, who
later wrote about the
problems with the
initial flower stand
scene. Note the flower
stand set in the
background

In fact, the initial meeting of the tramp and the flower girl constituted the most troublesome scene to shoot in the whole film. Granted, it's a delicate, complicated scene, essential to setting up a central relationship in the film. In it, the tramp has to recognise, without the use of dialogue, that the flower girl is blind, the flower girl must infer that the tramp is a wealthy man, and the scene must show that the characters are attracted to one another. All this must be communicated clearly to the audience.

One of the best accounts of the problems this scene caused is 'Working with Charlie Chaplin', by Egon Erwin Kisch, a Hungarian journalist who was introduced to Chaplin at the studio late one February afternoon by their mutual friend Upton Sinclair. Chaplin was agonising about how to make the scene work. Using Kisch as a test audience, he ran a rough cut of the scene, then became despondent when Kisch failed to understand some of its key ideas. Judging from Kisch's descriptions, he likely first visited on 11 or 12 February, staying around for a week or so, during which time Chaplin had failed to solve his problems.[48] In his autobiography Chaplin also recalls the problems the scene created, writing that 'the whole scene lasted seventy seconds, but it took five days of retaking to get it right'.[49] Kisch's account of the difficulties he observed is more accurate than Chaplin's memory, for the scene runs just short of three minutes in the final film, and the DPRs demonstrate that Chaplin took much longer to shoot the scene: after working on it for a month in February, he returned to it for more retakes than any other scene in the film. After the February failure, Chaplin returned five separate times: on 29 April 1929, from 30 December 1929 to 3 January 1930 (when he finally got some footage that made it into the finished film), and three more times in 1930 (on 29 August, 3–4 September, and 18 September). Two absolutely key shots in the scene (indeed, in the whole film) weren't shot until nearly the end of the shooting schedule. One – a pan left to a wealthy man getting into a car, continuing to a pan right past the tramp back to the flower girl, which shows that she mistakenly senses that the tramp is wealthy *and*

From the breakthrough shot of 4 September 1930. After the shot pans right, away from a wealthy man getting into a car that drives off, the flower girl and the tramp face the departing car. The tramp realizes that the flower girl believes he's the wealthy man

that the tramp notices her mistake and tiptoes away from her – was the last take after a long afternoon of shooting on 4 September 1930. The previous shot of the film – also important, for in it the tramp realises that the flower girl is blind and solicitously helps her sit down by the iron fence – was the sixth of nine takes on the afternoon of 18 September 1930. More than any other, this scene, and the frustrations it generated for Chaplin, justifies those who present the production of *City Lights* as an unrelentingly troubled time.

Furthermore, Chaplin's lack of progress on the film continued through much of 1929. On three occasions his frustrations resulted in actors being fired or replaced. Henry Clive, who had originally been cast as the millionaire after working on the set sketches of the film, was fired on 28 June after four days of shooting the river embankment scene when, for reasons of health, he refused Chaplin's request to jump into the water. Harry Myers replaced Clive as the millionaire, Chaplin reshot the scene between 1 and 5 July, generating some usable footage, and he continued to work well with Myers for the rest of the production.

However, production momentum slowed during the rest of July and into August 1928 because of hot weather and the widening of La Brea Avenue, which forced the reconstruction of some of the studio buildings facing the street. From 13 to 21 August, though, Chaplin worked hard on the 'chip' scene referred to earlier, in which the tramp tries to pry a stick loose from the pavement grate on the street corner. Apart from the opening scene, this required the most extras – between 100 and 110 on four of the days – and Harry Crocker, playing the man in the display window, was busy during much of the scene. Then production slowed again. Except for one day working on the nude statue scene, shooting would not resume again until 2 October, when Chaplin began the café sequence. More significantly, Harry Crocker was fired on 7 September. Crocker does not write about his dismissal in *Man and Mime*, nor does Chaplin, so the reasons for it remain unclear. However, we do know that Chaplin had included Crocker in story conferences from early on and that the production was beginning to seem directionless. The expensive 'chip' scene ultimately never made it into the film and remained unseen by the general public until its inclusion in the TV documentary series *The Unknown Chaplin*. Even worse, up to this point – over twenty months after the story conferences began, eight months after shooting began, and 874 takes into the production – only some footage from the opening scene and a few shots from the suicide sequence (itself reshot after Clive was fired) would make it into the final film. It's not unlikely that Chaplin felt the need for a creative change, and Crocker was the victim.[50]

Perhaps most significantly, on 11 November Chaplin fired Virginia Cherrill and hired Georgia Hale, who had played opposite Chaplin in *The Gold Rush*, to test for the part of the flower girl. During the previous week, Cherrill and Chaplin had been shooting two scenes between the tramp and the flower girl: the scene in which the tramp first takes the flower girl home, arriving in the millionaire's car, and the final shots of the film, outside the florist shop. Cherrill explained to interviewer Jeffrey Vance that she had left the studio grounds for lunch without Chaplin's permission and had returned five minutes late, keeping him waiting: 'We got into a screaming row and I was fired.'[51] The DPRs are silent on the reason for firing;

This enlargement is taken from Georgia Hale's screen test for the flower girl's role after Virginia Cherrill was fired (temporarily, as it turned out) in November 1929.

however, they suggest that Chaplin may also have been worried that the unknown actress he had hired for the key role of the flower girl wasn't up to the task. The DPR and the shooting notations from 11 November indicate that in the afternoon Cherrill and Chaplin shot nine retakes of what was to be the final shot of the film.[52] These were absolutely crucial moments in the film, and even if Chaplin was dissatisfied with the footage taken on the 10th and 11th (none of that footage makes it into the final film), he must have felt pretty desperate to contemplate firing Cherrill so far into the production. Surviving screen tests show Hale auditioning for the flower girl role by playing the final scene of the film; they make me, for one, yearn for Virginia Cherrill.[53]

10 The Production Clarifies: From November 1929

Fortunately, Chaplin reconsidered about a week later and asked Cherrill back. After her departure from the studio, she had been staying with actress Marion Davies at San Simeon. Because Cherrill had turned twenty-one after having signed the contract, Davies explained that her contract, signed as a minor, was now invalid and advised her to insist that Chaplin give her a pay rise. Chaplin was initially sceptical, but after checking with his lawyers, he offered to double Cherrill's salary from $75 to $150 a week, and by 21 November Chaplin and Cherrill were back shooting on the exterior set of the flower girl's home. They shot footage of the tramp escorting the flower girl up the stairs to her home on this day, and, significantly, much of it ended up in the finished film.

This constituted a crucial turning point in the production. Although shooting would continue for nearly eleven more months, the murkiness of the plot structure began to clarify in the coming weeks, and the extended desultory 'idle' periods, as in March and July/early August of 1929, vanished. Chaplin had finally settled on the performers for the other two key roles – the millionaire and the flower girl – and was beginning to work productively with both.

From this point on in the production, Chaplin worked with intensity and focus, concentrating at times on the flower girl's part of the narrative, then going back to the millionaire's story. After hiring Frances Lee to play the flower girl's grandmother on 27 November, Chaplin laboured on scenes with the flower girl and either the tramp or her grandmother through to 2 January 1930. After about two weeks of planning and preparing the sets, he went back to the millionaire plot, shooting the party scene in the millionaire's living room, the burglar sequence at the end of the film, and, by the middle

With its elaborate choreography and many extras, the boxing sequence was shot smoothly and efficiently, creating a party-like atmosphere on the set

of May, going on location early in the mornings to shoot scenes on the streets of Los Angeles of the millionaire and the tramp driving home after the cabaret party. Interspersed throughout this period were retakes designed to polish sequences that weren't yet quite right.

By mid-June, the production was running like a well-oiled machine. Hank Mann, who had worked with Chaplin as far back as the Keystone days, was hired on 12 June to play his boxing foe. Rehearsals began the next day, and the boxing-ring scene was shot between 23 and 30 June, followed by more rehearsals for the locker-room sequence, which was shot from 10 July through to the 21st. Virginia Cherrill remembered the shooting of the boxing-ring scene fondly:

Charlie must have had over a hundred extras present . . . and he encouraged his friends in town to come and watch. Everyone loved boxing in Hollywood in those days. And Charlie was so funny in the ring. The boxing scene became sort of a party at the studio. Charlie loved every minute of it.[54]

Unlike, say, the flower-stand scene where the tramp and flower girl first meet, the boxing and the locker-room scenes went smoothly for Chaplin and he didn't have to return to either location for retakes.

Shooting the boxing sequence must have reminded him of the old days, when he improvised on the set to make two-reel comedies like *The Champion* (1915), in which the tramp becomes a boxer.

Following the boxing sequence, for the last two months of shooting, Chaplin shot a few new scenes and did retakes of others to move smoothly toward the final cut. After some retakes of the burglar scene in the millionaire's living room, Chaplin returned to the flower girl's home. In the first half of August, he shot the scene in which the grandmother receives the rent-due notice, as well as the episode in which the tramp helps the flower girl wind the ball of yarn. He was satisfied enough to take Florence Lee, the grandmother, off contract on 20 August. Chaplin shot the tramp's arrest on 25 August, then quickly turned to retakes with the millionaire, shooting at the exteriors of the cabaret and the millionaire's home (where the millionaire fails to recognise the tramp and drives off), and the embankment suicide scene, after which Harry Myers was taken off contract on 5 September.

From 8 September, he stopped shooting for a week to plan what the DPRs call the 'New Flower Stand Scene' – the film's crucial final scene. Even though Chaplin had planned that scene very early in the scripting stage, he shot it at almost the very end of the production. Starting on Monday, 15 September, he was filming every day, except Sunday the 21st and Monday the 22nd. The last day was devoted to the final two shots of the film – the close-up of Virginia Cherrill (the shot that is divided by the title 'Yes, I can see now') and the last close-up of the tramp.

About a week's work remained. In two days Chaplin shot the scene in which the tramp gives the flower girl the money for her operation, then says he must go away. Another day took care of the scene outside the fight club where the tramp agrees to fight. Two more days at the street cleaners' shed knocked off Albert Austin's soap bubble gag. The 4 October DPR notes that Florence Lee had been recalled for some retakes of exchanges between the flower girl and her grandmother in the flower girl's home, and indicates tersely at the end of the report: 'Completed shooting on this picture today.' It seemed the long journey was over.

It was – or nearly so. Chaplin was both supervising the final editing and preparing the musical score, yet on 23 October he called back Virginia Cherrill and Florence Lee one more time. That afternoon he worked on three scenes: 1) the close-up of the tramp in the final scene when he asks, 'You can see now?'; 2) a new, brief scene between the flower girl and her grandmother after the tramp first takes the flower girl home, in which the grandmother says, 'He must be wealthy,' and the flower girl responds, 'Yes, but he's more than that'; and 3) the single shot of the tramp being led into jail following his arrest. After shooting the final retake of that scene, take 4,571 of *City Lights*, at 4:30 p.m., Chaplin and his crew officially packed up their gear. The shooting of *City Lights* was complete.

From the time he rehired Virginia Cherrill eleven months earlier, the production had run more smoothly, and Chaplin became increasingly sure of his aims in his 'Comedy Romance in Pantomime'. His productive work pace continued: he composed the score with music arranger Arthur Johnston and oversaw the recording by conductor Alfred Newman so fast that the film was ready for its preview audience on 19 January 1931. Now, what can we make of Chaplin's achievements in the completed film?

11 Chaplin, the Jazz Age, and Submerged Autobiography

Although *City Lights* was released as the United States was spiralling ever deeper into the Great Depression, Chaplin had developed its key conceptions – a romance between a blind flower girl and the tramp, a millionaire generous to the tramp when drunk and dismissive of him when sober, and the dynamics of the final scene – well before the stock market crash in October 1929. As such, it's not primarily a document of the 1930s: his most distinctive Depression-era film, *Modern Times*, would not appear until 1936. Rather, given the cultural context of the 1920s and Chaplin's personal experience of living through those years, *City Lights* is more properly considered Chaplin's farewell to that decade.

The 1920s in the United States were notable partly for three Republican presidential administrations and the economic prosperity that many – though not all – experienced, fuelled by expansion of consumer spending on products like automobiles, growth in advertising, encouragement of credit buying, and the confidence inspired by a rapidly climbing stock market. One strand of the decade, then, celebrated prosperity and materialism, even though that prosperity would be short-lived. A second strand was linked to an ethic of personal gratification and rejection of Victorian morality, symbolised by the flapper, the Charleston, and bootleg gin. That's the strain represented by F. Scott and Zelda Fitzgerald and their vaunted younger generation, and it's no surprise that Fitzgerald's 1922 collection of short stories, *Tales of the Jazz Age*, provided one of the designations of the decade that stuck. Those of the younger generation with enough wealth and leisure could join H. L. Mencken in mocking the 'Puritans' and 'booboisie'. They could also reject stuffed-shirt moralism and embrace instead an ethic of hedonism.

Yet many American storytellers, Fitzgerald included, were ambivalent about or highly critical of this celebration of materialism and a society of which President Coolidge could say, without a hint of irony, that 'the business of America is business'. Sinclair Lewis, who would later become the first American writer to win a Nobel Prize in Literature, provided the decade's most incisive satirical exposure of 'boosterism' in *Babbit* (1922). Written with the shadows of the Depression enveloping him, John Dos Passos wrote the third volume of his *U.S.A.* trilogy about America in the 1920s, *The Big Money* (1936). However, two of the most accomplished American novels of the decade invite particular comparison with *City Lights*: F. Scott Fitzgerald's *The Great Gatsby* and Theodore Dreiser's *An American Tragedy* (both 1925).

The two novels, like *City Lights*, are about love and money, set in a world in which social divisions exist and social class matters. In *The Great Gatsby* third-person narrator Nick Carraway tells the saga of Jay Gatsby, a man of humble Midwestern roots who rises to great wealth through questionable means, driven by the hope that he could – by accumulating wealth, possessions, and status – prove himself worthy of a woman he had fallen in love with, Daisy Buchanan. However, after their first flurry of romance, Daisy had rejected Gatsby's attentions and married Tom Buchanan, choosing status and security over love. Gatsby's dream of rekindling their love and reuniting with Daisy never comes to fruition. The novel ends with both an acknowledgment of the power of the American dream and a critique of how the power of that desire can lead to corruption and the confusion of ends and means. 'And so we beat on,' Fitzgerald concludes the novel, 'boats against the current, borne back ceaselessly into the past.'

Dreiser's *An American Tragedy* follows a similar line, focusing on the lure of wealth and the dream of upward mobility through love. Its protagonist, Clyde Griffiths, rejects his parents' fundamentalist evangelising, separates from his family as a young man, and is drawn to the promise of wealth and success represented by his uncle, factory owner Samuel Griffiths. Samuel, drawn to

Clyde's ambition, offers him a job. Clyde initially is attracted to Roberta Alden, the daughter of a farmer who also works in the factory, then turns his attentions to the beautiful, upper-class Sondra Finchley, a friend of Samuel's daughters. When Clyde learns that he has impregnated Roberta, however, he first obtains medications to abort her child. When those medications fail, he takes Roberta on a rowing-boat ride where, after the boat overturns, she drowns in the lake. Clyde is arrested for her murder, tried, convicted, and executed. Although Dreiser is ambiguous about Clyde's motivations in the rowing boat, his naturalism suggests that the forces of heredity and social class that shaped Clyde Griffiths, along with the trappings of fate, led to his demise. His dreams of love and money end in futility.

Like these two novels, *City Lights* revolves around love and money. Although early drafts of the script were not so clearly conceived, the finished film alternates cleanly between a world of romance, focused on the relationship between the tramp and flower girl, and a world of extreme wealth, focused on the millionaire and his interactions with the tramp. The first is associated more with women, the second is dominated by men. Flowers serve as the central visual emblem of the first world, while money defines the second world. Although Chaplin's film is partly a comedy and its ending is more open than the conclusions of *The Great Gatsby* or *An American Tragedy*, all three works engage with the power of romantic attraction and the dynamics of a world divided by those who have and those who do not.

These are powerful if not uncommon subjects in American literature and film, but the way they are developed in each work is profoundly influenced by the lives of each artist. Raised in a once-prosperous family of declining fortunes, Fitzgerald was in part meditating on his own experience of having his marriage proposal turned down by Zelda Sayre, daughter of a prominent Alabama judge. Only after his novel *This Side of Paradise* (1920) had become a critical and popular success did Zelda accept Fitzgerald's proposal. But the initial rejection had a powerful effect on his subsequent fiction, for he meditated on upward mobility, romantic rejection, and social class not just in *The Great Gatsby* but in short stories like 'Winter Dreams' and 'The Diamond as Big as the Ritz' (both 1922).

Dreiser's lower-middle-class background, in turn, informed his depiction of Clyde Griffiths. Son of a German immigrant and a farm girl of Czech ancestry, he experienced religious evangelising parents similar to Clyde's: Dreiser's father's business had failed two years before he was born, after which religion provided solace to his despair and poverty. Dreiser left home at sixteen, turned to journalism for a time, then began writing fiction. Yet he never forgot the struggle of poverty in a land of plenty, and even after he achieved a measure of success and acclaim as a novelist, he remained fascinated with the world of wealth and achievement, most often as observed from an outsider's perspective.

Chaplin's work is informed by autobiography, too, and the differences between his handling of love and money in *City Lights* may be linked to his unusual life experiences. Like Dreiser – and also like Dickens, whose work Chaplin's resembles in many ways – Chaplin knew vividly, through first-hand experience in childhood, the strains and challenges of family instability and poverty. Yet following his meteoric ascent in the movie industry during the mid-1910s, Chaplin shot directly into a world of wealthy celebrity that not even Fitzgerald would ever approach. Growing up a 'have not', Chaplin became a 'have' beyond his wildest dreams. And he learned that wealth and celebrity were double-edged swords: they granted him creative licence and freedom from want but also foreclosed anything like a truly 'private life'. He lived through the whole of the 1920s as just such a celebrity, and in *The Idle Class* (1921), which anticipates *City Lights* in various interesting ways, he explored indirectly the two vastly different social worlds he experienced by playing two roles: the tramp and a lonely man of wealth estranged from his wife.

I use the word 'indirectly' advisedly. Chaplin is not an overtly autobiographical artist as, for example, Fitzgerald in *Tender is the Night* (1934) – so closely does that novel parallel Fitzgerald's relationship to Zelda during her hospitalisation for psychological and emotional illness. Rather, Chaplin transforms his personal experiences and inclinations into 'submerged autobiography' in his films: in his movies he embeds in his characters – often more than one character in a film – sides of his own personality and experience.[55] The submerged autobiography is apparent, of course, in his alter ego, the tramp, whose marginal social status, resilience, and creative imagination are connected to the world of struggle, poverty, and, eventually, the work of performance he knew as a child and young adult. But it's also evident in other characters, like the ringmaster in *The Circus*: the imperious control he holds over his circus employees resembles the control Chaplin himself exerted as a film writer/ director after he rose to a position of financial security and creative independence. Although the autobiography in Chaplin's films is submerged, it is also deeply felt and rooted in his own highly unusual life experiences. And it helps to explain the emotional power of his best films, perhaps most memorably *City Lights*.

Like earlier films from the 1920s, including *The Kid*, *The Idle Class*, *A Woman of Paris*, and *The Circus*, Chaplin's farewell to the 1920s employs submerged autobiography in interesting ways, leading to the film's central concerns. For instance, his bitter divorce with Lita Grey Chaplin in 1927 and the death of his mother in August 1928 figure in the film in indirect ways. The divorce from Lita signalled his second failed marriage in less than a decade, yet it didn't turn Chaplin away from what had become a staple in his films: the tramp's romantic attraction to a woman, like Georgia in *The Gold Rush* and the horseback rider in *The Circus*. Yet *City Lights* differs from these two films: whereas they depicted the tramp experiencing unrequited love, it explores the possibilities of a mutual love relationship where, because of circumstances, a woman the tramp adores and makes sacrifices for also returns his affections. Partner in two failed marriages and a number of short-term relationships with women in the 1920s, Chaplin seems interested here in exploring how a mutual love relationship might work.[56]

That question, in turn, is inflected by the flower girl's blindness and thus linked to the death of Chaplin's mother. As an adolescent and a young man, Chaplin was frustrated at being unable to help his mother as she struggled with her physical and psychological afflictions. As I've noted, although he did provide support for Hannah when he was financially able, and brought her over to live her last years in California, his visits to her often left him despondent and unable to work. Her death, I'd argue, also played in complex ways into the development of the flower girl and the tramp's relationship to her.[57] Recall Jeffrey Vance's observation that in Chaplin's first film after Hannah's death, the tramp devotes himself to a woman with a physical impairment and finances her cure. Chaplin could perhaps, through the tramp, achieve in the fantasy world of art something he could never manage in the more intractable world of life.

Submerged autobiography also plays into the millionaire's character. Remember that Chaplin was a millionaire himself throughout the 1920s and, like the millionaire, his marriage had just crumbled the same year he started working on the story. That fractured marriage led to emotional strain and, if the newspaper reports were accurate, even a nervous breakdown. Kenneth Lynn suggests that Chaplin's friend Ralph Barton also serves as a source for the millionaire: Barton's 'bon-vivant appetites and tastes' were countered by his deep disillusionment when relationships with women failed, leading him to thoughts of suicide.[58] Like Barton and Chaplin, the millionaire, despite his wealth, fights despair and contemplates suicide because of failures in his relationships, and the tramp's optimistic advice to embrace life sounds remarkably similar to the advice offered by Sydney when Chaplin was facing his demons of despair amid the divorce proceedings. Take, too, the millionaire's alcoholism and the erratic behaviour that results from it. We need only to recall that alcoholism contributed to the early death of Chaplin's father, leaving Charlie deeply suspicious of alcohol his whole life. The millionaire thus contains some submerged autobiographical residue of Barton, of Chaplin himself, and of his father. Add to this the tramp character, always Chaplin's alter ego, rooted in the marginal world of society that Chaplin himself knew as a child, and you have the three central characters of *City Lights*: the blind flower girl, the millionaire, and the mediating tramp.

12 The Narrative Structure

Linked to *The Great Gatsby* and *An American Tragedy* as his
farewell to the 1920s, inflected by submerged autobiography, *City
Lights* represents Chaplin working at the height of his powers as a
film-maker at that crucial aesthetic moment of the early sound era.
After months of uncertainty, wrong turns, false starts, and obstinate
frustrations, Chaplin finally managed to tell a story of classical clarity
and simplicity revolving around the tramp and his movement
between the worlds of the flower girl – associated with flowers and
romance – and the millionaire – a masculine realm of money that
alternates between frenzied celebration and despair.

I noted above that in his films before *City Lights* Chaplin
worked out an 'aesthetic contract' with his audience that promised
five elements: 1) a central comic persona, the tramp; 2) a romance
between the tramp and the female lead; 3) inventive visual comedy;
4) integration of scenes that evoke pathos for the tramp or for
another sympathetic character; and 5) a narrative involving two
contrasting sets of values or moral perspectives. In this transitional
film, Chaplin's first feature after the introduction of sound, the
director continued to work within this framework. A good way to
begin to understand how the narrative of *City Lights* dovetails with
Chaplin's aesthetic contract is to divide the narrative into its
individual scenes.[59]

1 DAY ONE:
a) City square, morning – dedication of monument
b) Art store – tramp observes nude statue
c) Flower stand – tramp and flower girl (FG) meet for the first time
d) FG's home, evening (interior and exterior) – FG tells grandmother of her
    benefactor; at window, FG hears couple leaving on date

e) River embankment, night – tramp saves millionaire from suicide attempt

f) Millionaire's living room – tramp consoles despairing millionaire

g) Cabaret – millionaire and tramp celebrate

2 DAY TWO:

a) On streets, early morning (on-location exteriors) – millionaire and tramp drive home after party

b) Millionaire's home (interior hall, front exterior, on-location exterior) – tramp encounters FG, gets money from millionaire, buys flowers, drives FG home

c) FG's home (exterior) – tramp escorts FG home, observes her

d) Millionaire's home (interior hall, front exterior, on-location exterior) – tramp takes car to get cigar, millionaire rejects tramp

e) FG's home (interior) – FG talks to grandmother

f) Cabaret entrance, that afternoon (living room, side exterior) – tramp encounters drunk millionaire

h) Millionaire's home – the party (living room and side exterior)

3 DAY THREE:

a) Millionaire's home, the morning after (bedroom, guest bedroom, living room, front exterior) – tramp ejected

b) Flower stand – tramp seeks FG

c) FG's home (exterior and interior) – tramp discovers FG's illness

4 WORKING TO HELP FG:

a) City streets near monument – tramp works as street cleaner

b) FG's home (interior) – letter shows rent due, FG senses grandmother's distress

c) Street cleaner shed – lunch break, soap/cheese gag

d) FG's home (interior) – tramp visits at lunchtime, brings food, article on cure, helps wind yarn [single cutaway shot of grandmother at flower stand], finds letter, reads rent trouble to FG

e) Street cleaner shed – tramp fired for being late

5 BOXING SEQUENCE:

a) Exterior fight club – tramp gets boxing match
b) Locker room – first boxer leaves, second tougher boxer hired, tramp prepares for fight
c) Boxing ring – preliminaries, round one, dream of FG between rounds, round two, knockout
d) Locker room – tramp lies knocked out on table

6 REUNITING WITH MILLIONAIRE:

a) Cabaret entrance – tramp encounters millionaire
b) Millionaire's home, living room – tramp gets money, consoles millionaire, burglars attack and escape
c) Side exterior, tramp caught by policeman
d) Living room – millionaire denies tramp, who turns out lights and escapes
e) Side exterior, tramp directs policemen into living room, escapes

7 GIFT AND ARREST:

a) FG's home (exterior) – tramp arrives and (interior) gives money to FG, says he must leave
b) Art store corner – tramp arrested
c) Jailhouse exterior – tramp escorted in by officers
d) Calendar montage, January to autumn 1930

8 FINAL SEQUENCE:

a) Florist shop – FG in new prosperous setting
b) Flower stand – tramp trudges by, looking for FG
c) Florist shop – FG yearns for her benefactor's return
d) Street corner – newsboys shoot peas at tramp
e) Florist shop window – tramp sees FG observe him from inside shop
f) Outside florist shop door – tramp and FG's final interchange

As this segmentation suggests, in *City Lights* Chaplin tells a story that fulfils all five terms of his aesthetic contract. The tramp character so central to the film is introduced in the first scene, features in the last shot, and appears in most scenes in between. The romance between the flower girl and the tramp, which begins in scene 1c, constitutes a major narrative strand throughout the film, right up to the final scene. Inventive visual comedy is central to the film, most notably in such scenes as the monument dedication (1a), the cabaret scene (1g), the party at the millionaire's home (2h), the scene where the flower girl unwinds the tramp's underwear (4d), and the boxing scenes (5b and c). Besides these signature comedy scenes, the film is also filled with smaller yet memorable comic moments, as when the tramp – driving in the millionaire's car and wearing a tuxedo – jumps out of the car and onto the pavement to wrest a discarded cigar stub from a bum who's also spied it. Nevertheless, knowing as we do that the final scene was determined very early in the story development stage, one could argue that Chaplin structures the entire film around a final sequence designed to generate pathos. Finally, the contrasting worlds are clearly defined: the logic of the narrative, starting with the first meeting of the tramp and the flower girl in 1c, is to have the tramp move between two alternative moral universes represented by the flower girl and the millionaire. Furthermore, by having the tramp develop relationships with both characters, Chaplin presents the flower girl's world positively while critiquing the central tenets of the millionaire's world.

As a key transitional film in Chaplin's career, the narrative seems more integrated than in some of his earlier features, the handling of pathos more powerful. Although some have argued that *City Lights* is too episodic, Walter Kerr is persuasive when he writes that the film 'is the most ingeniously formed, immaculately interlocked of Chaplin's experiments in combining comedy with pathos. The comedy and the love story depend utterly on each other; neither can move until the other requires it to.'[60] Indeed, comedy often interrupts the spell of romance, as when the flower girl unknowingly douses the tramp with water in 1c, and a cat knocks a flower pot off a window sill onto the head of the romantically swooning tramp below in 2c.[61] Alternatively, comic scenes can take on romantic undertones, as when the tramp dreams of the flower girl in his corner between rounds one and two of the boxing match (5c). Or consider the embankment scene in which the tramp and millionaire first meet: it's about someone in such despair that he's attempting suicide, but its dominant tone is comic.

Furthermore, perhaps as a result of the painful emotional strains Chaplin had endured in the year before and during the production of the film – failure in his relationships, the death of loved ones – the stakes seem higher than in some of his earlier films. Gerald Weales suggests that through the presentation of the tramp and his romance with the flower girl, Chaplin was developing 'the most complex, the most painful treatment' of a theme he had already explored less fully in such earlier films as *The Kid*: 'the physical and psychological consequences of any attachment to another creature'.[62] Both the flower girl and the tramp yearn for love, but the flower girl's misapprehension and the tramp's vulnerable social marginality, despite his selfless and whole-hearted commitment to her, lead inexorably to the complexity and pain that Weales describes.

The narrative structure is quite simple, even if complex within that simplicity. Put most simply, it first establishes the tramp as a central character, then places him between the world of the flower girl and the world of the millionaire, two moral universes that contrast one another in distinctive ways. The film begins in 1a and 1b by establishing the tramp's character. From there we alternate between the flower girl's world and the millionaire's world from sections 1c and 1d – where the romance begins – through to section 3a, when the millionaire prepares to leave for Europe. Upon his departure, the tramp seeks out the flower girl, learns first of her illness and then of her difficulty with the rent. After the tramp's empathy for her is intensified and his motivation to make money established, the film alternates between scenes in the flower girl's world and the tramp's attempts to make money to help her, through the boxing sequence in section 5. Upon the millionaire's return, sections 6 and 7 take the tramp to the millionaire's world, then back to the flower girl's world, where he gives her the money and they part, after which he is promptly arrested and summarily imprisoned. The final sequence reunites the tramp and the flower girl in the new circumstances – his abjection and her prosperity – leading to the famous ending. With this general structure in mind, let's look more closely at how Chaplin develops the narrative through his stylistic choices.

Space considerations make any close analysis of the whole narrative impossible. Rather, I would like to look at the opening scenes (1a–c) in some detail to see how they introduce first the tramp, then the flower girl and their romance; turn to a more general discussion of how Chaplin differentiates between the flower girl's world and the millionaire's world through the use of film form; then conclude with a close analysis of how the blend of narrative and cinematic style helps lead to the powerful emotional effects of the film's last sequence (8a–f).

13 The Opening Scenes: A Closer Look

The two opening scenes of *City Lights* – the monument and the nude statue scenes – define the tramp's marginal social status and help establish his character before he begins alternating between the contrasting worlds of the flower girl and the millionaire. As the film opens, people crowd into a city square, waiting for the public dedication of a new monument, 'Peace and Prosperity', which is covered by a tarpaulin. The scene takes place in the 'city set' of the film, located just north of the garage and dressing rooms at the Chaplin studio (see pages 33 & 42). In fact, most of the scenes in the film that show the exteriors of city buildings, including the famous final scene, were shot in this location.

Before the tramp even appears, however, Chaplin establishes his aesthetic rejection of talking films through his presentation of the public figures on the stage where the monument is to be dedicated. When a rotund bald official in formal dress (Henry Bergman) begins addressing the crowd, an annoying kazoo-like noise plays on the soundtrack. The same effect is employed, but at a higher pitch, to accompany an older, thin woman in a frilly dress and feathered hat and again – the pitch now lowered – for a bespectacled white-haired man who seems to repeat 'thank you' three times. By using sound effects rather than language, Chaplin mocks the platitudes of politicos and do-gooder elites, simultaneously refusing to let talk overwhelm the visual aesthetics of silent film comedy.

He does, however, use music. Fast-paced background strings – later used during some of the boxing sequence – play beneath the kazoo speeches. Then, accompanied by a brass fanfare, the upper-class woman tugs on a ribbon, prompting the tarpaulin to be lifted from the monument. Beneath it, we see the tramp, the antithesis of prosperity, sleeping on the lap of the middle of three figures. A more

'Peace and Prosperity' Monument

careful look at the monument emphasises how ridiculous the figuration of 'Peace and Prosperity' really is. The central figure, a woman, sits in a chair, forearms resting on the arms. The other two figures, males in togas, are oddly posed: the figure on screen left has raised his right hand, holding it open, palm facing the crowd. The left arm, bent at elbow, reaches to his left, hand held open, as if expecting a tip from passers-by. The other figure lies on the ground, resting on his left elbow, with his right arm extended at a 45-degree angle, the sword extending outward from the hand. It's unclear just who is peace and who is prosperity. As the tramp awakens, he scratches first his head, then the inside of his right thigh. When the crowd gestures for him to get off the monument, fast foxtrot music begins to play.

As the tramp tries to get off the statue, away from the irate crowd, the mystifying monument suddenly acquires a function, becoming a gag machine highlighting the tramp's earthy roots and social marginality, as well as the hostility of the well-heeled to the have-nots. The tramp first gets his trousers hung up on the sword wielded by the male figure on the right when trying to dismount from the woman's lap. When 'The Star Spangled Banner' begins to play, he takes off his derby and does his best to stand to attention, even while suspended from the sword.[63] Slipping off the sword, he slides down

the arm right into the statue's face, then crosses to the other side of
the monument and uses that statue's right hand to thumb his nose to
the crowd. Both images suggest the tramp's marginal, anarchic spirit,
rooted in the Keystone days; yet elements of costume – derby, polka-
dotted bow tie, cane – and gestures such as trying to stand at
attention while the national anthem is being played and tipping his
hat to acknowledge the crowd suggest the tramp's gentlemanly side,
too – a dimension of the character that has also been evident from the

Charlie inadvertently
sits on the first statue
and uses the second to
'thumb his nose' to
the crowd

mid-1910s on. Finally, after manoeuvring to the back of the statue, screen right – carefully slipping by the pointed tip of the sword – the tramp exits as plucked harp strings indicate the end of the scene.

The next scene further develops the tramp's character. A title card says 'Afternoon', and the 'Promenade' musical motif that plays at least seven times in the film, most often when the tramp is strolling along city streets, begins. The set is a street corner, with a music store in the foreground, a theatre and, to its left, a news and tobacco store across the street in the background.[64] As people hurry along the pavement, the tramp saunters to the corner, places his cane under his arm, and turns to his left. As he walks off, a newsboy on the corner grabs the hook of his cane. When the tramp turns back to retrieve it and scold the newsboy by pointing his finger, the boy pulls the detached finger off the tramp's glove. The tramp tries to maintain an aura of respectability but then has to pull off the detached middle glove finger to snap his fingers at the boys. Because some of this episode is framed more tightly than the opening scene, the medium shots reveal that Charlie's respectable costume is a bit the worse for wear. The coat is too tight, the plaid vest frayed, the pants baggy, the gloves threadbare: if the music suggests the tramp is a gentleman, the costume reinforces the notion but suggests that he's fallen on hard times. While in the opening scene policemen and city elites chase the tramp, here two lowly street urchins make fun of him, further emphasising his isolation and social marginality. Nonetheless, his cane retrieved, the tramp continues walking right, past a 'danger' sign to the front of an art store display window that contains a small statue of a man holding the reins of a spirited horse and a life-size statue of a nude woman.

The film then cuts from the exterior of the art store to a reverse view from its interior. In the foreground we see the rear of the statues, the tramp in mid-range, and a men's furnishings store in the background.[65] This shot – which constitutes the rest of the scene and the second longest take of the film at 83 seconds – is a brilliant exercise in character study, then suspense, then social dynamics.[66]

The tramp as art connoisseur, unaware of the danger that lurks just behind him

The tramp first assumes the air of an art connoisseur, looking at the horse statue, but then steals a brief glance at the nude. It's amusing to see his attention shifting back and forth: eventually, the beauty of the female form overwhelms the tramp's attention, and he directs his attention more fully to the figure of the female body by backing away from the window to take in the whole view.

The tramp's backward movement adds the layer of suspense to the scene. Unbeknown to the tramp, a delivery hoist lies directly behind him, and it moves up and down as he's studying the statue. As he continues his contemplation of aesthetic beauty in the long take, he moves backwards and forwards, and barely avoids tumbling into the hole, stepping onto the hoist just as it reaches ground level. One of a number of beautifully choreographed long takes in the film (several shots in the boxing scene also come to mind), the shot echoes the teetering cabin in *The Gold Rush* and anticipates the tramp's blind roller-skating scene in the department store in *Modern Times*: in all three we fear for the tramp's well-being as he moves close to disaster and are relieved when he just manages to avoid it.

The shot ends, though, when the tramp realises the danger and turns on the worker operating the hoist. Having backed onto the hoist while it's at pavement level, the tramp is shocked when it starts

The tramp scolds the workman for endangering him

moving down. Quickly he clambers up to street level, and as he looks down the hole, he sees a man emerging when the hoist moves part way up. Indignant at the danger he's faced and the workman's carelessness, the tramp points his finger at the workman in a righteous scolding manner. However, the hoist then rises to ground level – while an oboe plays four dropping notes – to reveal that the workman is at least a head taller than the tramp. The music halts, as if to give the tramp a chance to reconsider. As resilient and pragmatic as ever, the tramp steps back, looks up, assesses the situation, tips his hat, and, as the music resumes, takes a wide berth around the workman and walks off.

By the end of these opening two scenes, we have a firm sense of the tramp's social status and character. On the one hand, he's homeless and at the outer fringes of society, criticised not just by city elites and policemen but even by lowly newsboys. On the other hand, his costume and behaviour – and even the 'Promenade' theme that will often accompany him on the city streets – suggest a certain refinement, or at least an aspiration to gentility. He stands at attention – or at least tries to – when the national anthem plays, while his response to the artworks suggests both aesthetic appreciation and an attraction to female beauty. He's not a 'big bad wolf' masculine stereotype – strong, dominating, handsome, and brash – like the Clark Gable character in Capra's *It Happened One Night* (1934). His aesthetic sense and diminutive stature give him a gentler, almost feminised dimension.[67] In addition, the tramp possesses an ethical sense, knowing it's not right to expose himself (and others) to danger and willing to express that perspective forcefully. Yet his morality is tempered by a pragmatic realisation of his place in the world: when it becomes clear that his denunciation of the worker may put him in physical danger, the tramp backs down, courteously tips his hat, and scurries away from danger. He may be alone, he may be marginal, he may not fit dominant conceptions of masculinity, but he's smart enough to be a survivor.

The tramp's character established, we move to the flower girl and the world of romance. As we have seen, the film's third scene (1c) caused Chaplin enormous difficulty – the scene's fourteen shots (not counting the two intertitles) were filmed over a long period of time (see Section 9). Yet the finished product manages to communicate efficiently several complex yet crucial ideas: that the flower girl is blind, that the tramp recognises this, that she believes the tramp is wealthy, and that he is aware that she believes this. In addition, the scene skilfully introduces the mood of budding romance.

Chaplin establishes two key motifs of the flower girl's world with the first shot of the scene: the prop of flowers and the central romantic musical motif in the film – Jose Padilla's 'La Violetera'.[68] As a close-up of a large basket of carnations and roses fades in at the start of the scene, the opening bars of 'La Violetera' begin to play. Three in-camera dissolves follow: a close-up of the blind flower girl, then a medium long shot, and finally a long shot, in which the flower girl sits at her stand on the right of the frame while an elegant chauffeur-driven car, otherwise empty, pulls up to the kerb on the left. As that fourth image comes to an end, the first stanza of 'La Violetera' is complete.

The melody is repeated four more times, with variations in rhythm, instrumentation, and volume emphasising different elements throughout the scene. The tramp, winding through crowded traffic, enters and then walks through the back seat of the limousine, stepping onto the pavement and slamming the door behind him. He's surprised when the flower girl solicits a tramp like him to buy a flower, particularly after the scorn he's faced earlier in the day, yet he walks toward her and points to the carnation in her right hand. As she offers him the carnation, the tramp accidentally knocks it from her grasp with his elbow. He picks it up but is puzzled when the flower girl drops to her knees to seek it herself, then asks in a title card, 'Did you pick it up, sir?' In response the tramp first looks annoyed, but when he places the carnation in front of her eyes and sees no response, his sympathetic and gentlemanly demeanour take over. The music emphasises his realisation by slowing the rhythm of 'La Violetera' as he becomes aware of her blindness, then tips his hat, places the flower in her hand, and reaches his other hand to her elbow to help her stand.

As the flower girl pins the carnation to his lapel, the tramp gazes longingly into her face. In the first of several such gestures, he gently grasps her hand and places a coin in it, then helps her sit down by her change box. As she sits, Chaplin cuts to an intricate long shot as the tramp's left hand slides away from the flower girl's

Recognizing her blindness, the tramp is smitten by the flower girl's beauty and kindness

elbow. In the shot, Chaplin pans left as a wealthy man in a top hat walks past the tramp, opens the same car door that the tramp had earlier walked through, steps in, and slams it. The camera then pans right, back to the flower girl, and cuts to a title card – 'Your change, sir?' – as the music lingers on one note. As the shot resumes and the flower girl reaches her hand toward the car, Chaplin again pans left, showing the tramp looking at the car, then pans back right as he returns his gaze to the flower girl, after which both look toward the departing car (see page 46). The shot, aided by the rhythm of the music, communicates clearly that the flower girl believes the tramp is a wealthy man and that the tramp realises her assumption, for then he slowly tiptoes away and around the corner.

However, he can't resist coming back to sit next to the fountain and admire her beauty. As he does so, the last of the five variations of 'La Violetera' begins. The flower girl unknowingly walks in front of him to the fountain, where she begins rinsing out a container with water while the tramp gazes on. In the first of many such comic deflations of romance (and romantic extensions to comedy), Chaplin pauses the music completely while the flower girl swirls water in the container, then tosses the water out directly into the tramp's face. Chaplin the composer here resists the temptation to emphasise the comedy with loud music, relying on pantomime alone to generate the humour. As the romantic theme returns and its fifth variation concludes, the love-smitten but soaked tramp quietly tiptoes out of the frame screen left.

14 Contrasting Moral Universes

While the opening three scenes introduce the tramp, the flower girl, and the possibility of romance, the third also begins to set up the contrast between two moral universes – the flower girl's world and the millionaire's world – that takes up much of the rest of the narrative up to the final sequence. In its portrayal of these two contrasting worlds and sets of values, *City Lights* differs from earlier Chaplin films. Some, like *The Kid*, presented the tramp as the source of the positive values, and those who opposed him, like the charity officials who try to take the kid from him, as the source of negative values. In *City Lights*, however, the flower girl's world generally contains life-affirming value; although hers is a world of bare economic subsistence, it is also a world of family support, simplicity, belief in tradition, and the possibility of mutually committed, loving relationships. In contrast, the millionaire's world – the world of city lights – is for the most part much more negative; although one of economic prosperity, it is also a schizophrenic world, shifting between celebration and coldness, welcoming inclusion and harsh exclusion, alcoholic camaraderie and suicidal sobriety. In moving between these two worlds and interacting in charitable ways with both the flower girl and the millionaire, the tramp experiences both sets of values. Over the course of the film, Chaplin affirms the flower girl's world and challenges that of the millionaire.

Chaplin develops these contrasting worlds in part through *mise en scène* – sets and props, costumes, and acting styles – buttressed by the musical score. The flower girl's world is defined most clearly through the apartment she lives in with her grandmother: the wooden-floored room, simply furnished, combines kitchen, dining room, and living room in one space. Dishes sit on the table and in the cupboard at the back left of the screen while the grandmother prepares tea and slices bread. Although the space is tight and the furnishings modest,

The home of the flower girl and her grandmother includes one room that combines kitchen, dining room, and living room

the room also exudes warmth: the fireplace adds a cozy glow, the checked tablecloth is homey, and the Victrola suggests that the pair enjoy listening to music. Visible to the right of the Victrola is a photo album that has an honoured place on the table: later in the film Charlie gets it from the table to look at the family pictures, only to be interrupted when the rent-due letter falls out of it. Besides what is visible in this image, we later learn that there is a bedroom off screen left, while a window at screen right enables the flower girl to face the courtyard as she waters the potted flowers. That the photo album should be treated with respect and that the flower girl and her grandmother care for live potted flowers is significant. As we shall see, the millionaire's world is set in stark contrast to this warm haven.

Like her surroundings, the flower girl's clothing is modest: she wears a sweater over her simple longish dress, and dark stockings cover her legs. With her long-sleeved blouse, long skirt, apron, and shawl, the grandmother seems to belong more to a Victorian novel – or to Chaplin's memories of Hannah – than a film set in the Jazz Age. The costumes also suggest their social class: they are poor, but they also work to support themselves, selling a product that they hope will enrich the lives of their customers who buy their flowers even if it doesn't promise wealth for the sellers. Moreover, the comfortable,

The courtyard outside the flower girl's apartment has a European feel and is more a site for community than the city spaces depicted in the millionaire's world. Note the potted plants in three windows, as well as the cat and the barrel, both sources for gags

relaxed, and loving way that the flower girl and her grandmother interact with one another indicates their fulfilling and warm relationship, just as their costumes do.

Outside the flower girl's apartment lies a courtyard that also gives us a sense of her world. This site suggests both community and the possibility of love. People who live within this space seem to have forged a community. When the flower girl first arrives home after meeting the tramp, for example, two younger girls greet her. Later, when she waters the plants and looks out of the window, she hears a young couple meet to depart for a date at the base of the stairs; as 'La Violetera' plays on the soundtrack, both greet her kindly, and the close-up of her response as they walk away suggests she's yearning, too, for a romantic relationship. Later, the same space provides the site for one of the most romantic images in the film: when the tramp first drives the flower girl home after using the millionaire's money to buy all her flowers, he reaches for her hand – clasped hands constituting a key visual motif in the film – and kisses it as they both stand on the stairway. This place of community, family, and the possibility of love is crucial to establishing what Weales argues is a central concept of *City Lights* – the tramp's willingness to make himself vulnerable by connecting himself fully to another person in a selfless way.

The millionaire's living room contrasts to the flower girl's home in spaciousness, lavish furnishings, and impersonality. Note the photograph of the millionaire's estranged wife in a kind of showgirl pose at the left of the frame. The millionaire later unceremoniously throws it aside

The *mise en scène* of the millionaire's world tells quite another story. Significantly, we first encounter the millionaire at the river embankment where he's planning to drown himself; ironically, it provides a sombre setting that generates loads of comic business as the tramp nearly drowns trying to prevent the millionaire from committing suicide. We get a stronger sense of the millionaire's world, however, when he takes the tramp home. His living room contrasts to the flower girl's apartment in almost every way. Much larger than the flower girl's whole apartment, it's elegantly and expensively furnished, with a grand piano, other fine furniture, luxurious drapes, elaborate moulding, and thick carpets. However, it is not a place of happiness: when the tramp and millionaire first enter the room, the millionaire learns from his valet that his wife has left him. Walking screen left, he picks up the picture of his wife and heedlessly slings it aside, a stark contrast to the reverence with which the photo album is treated in the flower girl's world. Note, too, the lack of any living plants or flowers in the living room – again a contrast to the warmth and affirmation of life in the flower girl's world. (Indeed, at one point when the millionaire wakes up sober on the couch and sees in his lap the large bouquet of flowers the tramp bought from the flower girl, he merely brushes them aside.) The

The two bedroom sets in the millionaire's mansion are both simply redressings of the millionaire's living room set. Note especially the arched windows and the molding around and between the windows

millionaire once more threatens suicide by pulling out a handgun (the tramp again dissuades him) and throws a party that lasts until the next morning: like the millionaire's personality, the living room is alternately a site of suicidal distress and hedonistic celebration. Finally, the room is only a small part of his mansion: in other scenes we see his bedroom, an adjoining bedroom where the tramp gets ready to leave after the sobered-up millionaire orders him out of the house, and a hallway that goes from the living room to the front door.[69] Although his living spaces reflect his economic security, they also paradoxically provide the space where, if he's not partying, he displays his loneliness, despair, and lack of concern for other people.

The costumes and acting styles of the millionaire's world also contrast to those of the flower girl's. The millionaire nearly always wears formal attire, although whether his clothing looks impressive or dishevelled depends on his degree of sobriety. The other men and even the tramp – when he celebrates at the cabaret or goes to the millionaire's party – also wear formal dress.[70] The women in this world dress very differently from the flower girl: their dresses are expensive, usually sleeveless and often with deep necklines or backlines, and tend to be either floor length or considerably shorter than the flower girl's dress. Many also wear expensive necklaces or other jewellery. And the acting style of people in the millionaire's world – as typified in the cabaret scene or the party in his living room – is active, even frenzied, intensified by the fast foxtrot or other lively music that accompanies the parties. The millionaire's behaviour, appropriate to his character, is friendly and expansive when he's drinking but curt, rude, and dismissive when he's sober.

Parallel to the courtyard in the flower girl's world is the front of the millionaire's mansion. However, its lines and layout suggest

Costumes of both men and women at the Millionaire's party contrast starkly to the costumes in the flower girl's world. Note the women's sleeveless dresses, often cut low in front or back, and the woman clad even more scantily behind the formally attired tramp. The bald man on the lower right is the source of one of the scene's funniest gags

The exterior of the millionaire's home is elegant with the elaborate ironwork and fancy entrance lamps. However, it also suggests exclusion with the sharp lines, iron fences, and heavily protected door. This scene is the closest the flower girl gets to the millionaire: drunk, he agrees to let the tramp take her home in his car.

exclusion rather than community. The vertical and horizontal lines are sharp and distinct, in contrast to the smoother, rounder, softer courtyard of the flower girl's home.[71] Significantly, the millionaire's house is fenced in, and the iron fence is topped by sharp spikes that warn intruders to stay away. Note, too, the elaborate ironwork in the windows and doors: they suggest both great wealth and security concerns. Even if the windows in the door were smashed, the ironwork would make entrance difficult. Thus, even the architecture contributes to the millionaire's isolation and loneliness.

At this location the tramp becomes both beneficiary and victim of the millionaire's whims. In the image above, the tramp has bought the flower girl's entire stock of flowers and given her a ride home in the millionaire's car – drunk, the millionaire is generous to the tramp, enabling him to maintain the flower girl's illusion that he's wealthy. At two other times, though, the sober yet hungover millionaire denies the tramp and orders him to be tossed unceremoniously out of the front door. When he comes to his senses after a night of revelry, the millionaire's generosity dissolves, his friendship fizzles, and the dark, cold truth of his despair sets in. The *mise en scène* of his world visually embodies the quality of his life, just as the flower girl's embodies hers.

From the time he meets the flower girl in 1c until he's thrown into jail in scene 7c, the tramp moves back and forth between the two worlds of the flower girl and the millionaire, sidetracked only into the world of work when the millionaire leaves him and he tries to earn money to help the flower girl, first as a street cleaner, then as a boxer.[72] Throughout he interacts primarily with the flower girl and the millionaire, exhibiting a kind of nobility of behaviour with both. Mistaken for a wealthy gentleman in his first meeting, he treats the flower girl with generosity (thanks to the millionaire's largesse when he's drunk), kindness, and self-sacrificing concern. And the flower girl is drawn to him not simply because she thinks him to be rich. That's clear from the last scene written and shot in the film (2c), the brief exchange between the flower girl and her grandmother on the same day the tramp drives the flower girl home after buying all her flowers. When the grandmother says he must be wealthy, the flower girl replies in a title, 'Yes, but he's more than that.' In their mutual kindness and concern for one another, the flower girl and the tramp offer a model of romance and love that Chaplin was striving to depict and affirm in the film, even as it had eluded him up to that point in his life.

The tramp also seeks to treat the millionaire in a positive manner, but he's stymied by the millionaire's erratic behaviour. Persuading the despondent millionaire not to end his life by drowning in the embankment scene or by gunshot in his own living room, the tramp offers the promise of simple pleasures such as 'Tomorrow the birds will sing'. Although the millionaire does respond at one point to the tramp's encouragement by asserting 'I want to live', what he means by living is not enjoying bird songs the next morning but, rather, throwing himself back into the lights of the city by celebrating at the cabaret or hosting a party at home. In both cases, living means going back to drink, which leads him back to a hangover, which leads to another rejection of the tramp who saved his life. In one of the best sustained discussions of the moral implications of *City Lights*, Gerard Molyneaux writes that the millionaire 'is too drunk with the city's whiskey, deafened by its jazz, and jaded by its night life to listen' to the tramp's words. 'Were he sober,' Molyneaux continues, 'he would dismiss them with the same irritability with which he throws flowers from his lap, pictures to the floor, and good-hearted tramps out the door. . . . He is delighted and doomed by the distractions of the city.'[73] If the tramp tastes the possibility of mutual love in his relationship with the flower girl, he also experiences through his interactions with the millionaire the inauthenticity, shallowness, and despair of that city lights world. Chaplin's critique of this world is locked in when the tramp himself is locked up in scene 7c, accused of stealing the money that the drunken millionaire freely gave him. But *City Lights* does not end there. The final encounter between the tramp and the flower girl remains.

15 Final Sequence: Part One

I began by quoting James Agee's assertion that the final shots of *City Lights* are enough to 'shrivel the heart'. Chaplin's blend of narrative and cinematic style in the final sequence helps lead up to the emotional power of the ending and poses the movie's themes in sharp relief, even as it refuses the temptations of a closed ending. In the next two sections, let's examine more closely the film form of the final sequence, looking first at the alternating scenes 8a–d, then concentrating on what happens after the tramp first sees the flower girl again in 8e and f.

Music contributes fundamentally to the effect of the whole film, and never more so than in the final sequence. Although Chaplin had co-compiled film scores with various musical directors for his earlier feature films using pre-existing concert music, as was the general practice at the time, *City Lights* was, according to Timothy Brock, Chaplin's first 'through-music score', consisting largely of original music he had written with the assistance of his 'musical associate', Arthur Johnston. It was also his first recorded film score, conducted by newcomer Alfred Newman.[74] Brock, who has restored the music of the original *City Lights* score, notes that Chaplin wrote it for a large dance orchestra of no more than thirty-four instruments and that the 'notational ornamentation' of the score exhibits 'incredible delicacy'.[75] The final sequence illustrates well how Chaplin uses music to develop the narrative and intensify the emotional tone of the film.

The final sequence begins with a title card that reads simply 'Autumn', reminding us that the tramp has been in jail since early January, incarcerated for stealing the money that he received from the drunken millionaire, who in turn denied having done so when he regained consciousness following the burglar's attack.[76] Recall that just before he is captured and jailed, the tramp visits the flower girl's apartment and, in a touching scene, gives the grateful girl money for the overdue rent and for her eye surgery. A careful viewer will note the hand motif in this scene: the tramp twice clasps the flower girl's hand and kisses it, while she embraces and kisses his hands once. Even though the tramp exhibits his pragmatic, even endearingly larcenous, side by holding back one of the bills the millionaire gave him, when the flower girl shows her gratitude by kissing the back of his hand, he relents and gives her all the money, calling to mind a similar scene in *The Immigrant* (1917). The hand motif and the tramp's melancholy expression when, as he's about to leave, the flower girl asks him if he'll return, help set up the intricate and poignant reunion in the final scene.

In the first half of the final sequence, Chaplin contrasts the flower girl's new world with the tramp's now much-degraded condition by twice alternating between a scene of the flower girl, then a scene of the tramp. We start with the flower girl. As the 'Autumn' title card flashes on the screen, 'La Violetera' begins playing again, for the sixth time in the film. First played during the initial meeting between the flower girl and tramp, 'La Violetera' is associated with romance and their love, played when the tramp thinks of the flower

The tramp's response when, as he departs after bringing money to the flower girl for her surgery, she asks him if he will return to her

In an effective gesture, Chaplin has the flower girl look in the mirror to check on her hair as a way to verify that her sight has been restored. Note, too, she's nearer the world of men and money. A cigar store is in the background, as is the cabaret where the millionaire twice encounters the tramp

girl (for example, at the end of the embankment scene, when he returns for the carnation), when she dreams of love (for example, as she hears the couple leave for their date), and when they are together. Here it's played moderato and with a tambourine for the first time, conveying a livelier feel. On the screen we see the flower girl in medium shot, now dressed more elegantly but still modestly in a black dress with white lace collar, working on a floral arrangement in her prosperous shop across the street from the tobacco store and the theatre – spaces aptly associated with men, the millionaire, and city lights – assisted by her grandmother (now better dressed, too) and another female assistant. Although still associated with flowers, the flower girl is now closer to the world of money and prosperity, to the world of city lights.

Her improved situation established, Chaplin cuts to the park set for a long one-shot scene. Rounding the corner by the flower stand is the tramp. Although the prosperity of the city swirls around him as cars and stylish pedestrians pass by, the tramp – in long shot, dwarfed in the frame – looks beaten down. He moves slowly, slumps. His costume has deteriorated: his cane is gone, as are his bow tie and vest, even his shirt, and his baggy pants are torn at the turn-up, split halfway up to his knees. The left pocket of his trousers and both

Released from jail, the despondent tramp checks to see if the flower girl is still selling flowers on the corner

elbows bear sizeable rips, his coat collar turns up. Although 'La Violetera' begins again just as he rounds the corner, this time it's played andante – slightly slower – and in a lower key than in the previous scene, without the lightening effects of the castanets and tambourine, as befits his diminished condition. After the tramp checks the space and finds no evidence of the flower girl, he exits screen left.

The tables, clearly, are turned. The poor and blind but generous-spirited flower girl is now sighted and on a path to prosperity; the benefactor who made her new condition possible, and whom she believed to be a kind and wealthy man, is now more destitute than ever. Yet before the two meet, Chaplin continues symmetrically, returning to the flower girl and then again to the tramp, and in doing so brings to mind earlier moments in the film. We return to the floral shop, and a chauffeur-driven car pulls up, much like the one the tramp walked through in the first flower-stand scene. As a tall, slender young man in tuxedo, ascot, and top hat walks into the shop, 'La Violetera' resumes in moderato, in a higher register and accompanied once more by the castanets and tambourines. The flower girl looks up expectantly, but appears disappointed when he orders flowers and leaves; she then tells her grandmother that she thought her benefactor had returned. The scene clarifies for viewers how the flower girl imagines the tramp, making the disparity between her image and his present condition even more distinct, more painful.

From there Chaplin cuts to the corner, where two newsboys are hawking their wares, the same pair that teased him in scene 1b.[77] As the camera pans right to reveal the tramp slowly walking left past the music store, the orchestra shifts to the 'Promenade' theme, already played six times, usually, as we have seen, when the tramp was wandering the streets of the city. Earlier the theme had given the tramp a leisurely and gentlemanly air, but here the pace is slower than usual and the register lower: the violins start with an open G, the lowest note on the instrument. Part of the building power of the final sequence emerges in the way the music – alternating from scene to scene – deepens the disparity between the new circumstances of the tramp and the flower girl. As this more sombre 'Promenade' theme plays, the camera presents several shot/reverse shots between the boys and the dispirited tramp: one of the newsboys takes out a straw and shoots peas at the tramp, hitting him three separate times as he rounds the corner. The tramp protests half-heartedly and moves in front of the florist shop. The spring is gone from his step, the enthusiasm from his demeanour. As he turns to protest the final time, the flower girl's assistant emerges from the shop and sweeps some litter into the gutter. The tramp looks down, the music pauses briefly, and the film turns to its final passage – the reunion of the tramp and the flower girl, and their mutual recognition.

16 Final Sequence: The Heartbreaking Ending

As Chaplin cuts to an eyeline match from the tramp's point of view, showing a close-up of a fading rose that has been swept up by the kerb, 'La Violetera' returns for the last time, first played by three violins, shortly after joined by three more. After spying the rose, the tramp bends down to pick it up, and the second newsboy continues the torment by yanking his handkerchief from a rip in the back of his pants. As the flower girl and her assistant look on, the tramp responds more vigorously, grabbing back the handkerchief, then rushing after the newsboy and kicking out at him. The music briefly rests as the tramp holds out the handkerchief, then blows his nose, folds up the handkerchief, and places it in his front coat pocket. As all this happens, the flower girl and her assistant, looking on from inside the flower shop, react with amusement (See page 9). Knowing the crucial role the tramp has played in the flower girl's improved situation, her response, which borders on flippant, pains us.

Chaplin cuts to a medium shot of the tramp and the flower girl framed behind her, inside the shop. 'La Violetera' ends and, as the tramp turns and sees the flower girl for the first time in the scene, the score pauses: Chaplin displays here, as he has earlier in the film, an intuitive understanding of how silence, too, can create a point of emphasis in a recorded soundtrack. As their eyes lock, a beautiful violin recitative begins, framed by the rest of the string section with a harp obbligato, and plays for 70 seconds, until the flower girl grasps the tramp's hands outside the store.[78] The interplay between the tramp and the flower girl during the start of this segment – consisting of three shot/reverse shots – is both emotionally complex and thematically resonant. When he first sees the flower girl, the tramp registers a look of surprise, which slides into a warm smile. Chaplin cuts to a medium close-up of the flower girl, who laughs and turns to her assistant, joking in a title card, 'I've made a conquest.' Although her face doesn't convey a callous spirit, the viewer reading the deeply ironical comment still is invited to empathise with the tramp. We cut back to the reverse angle, the tramp – outside the window, deaf to the comment – still smiling, although the rose he's holding begins dropping its petals, an objective correlative for a fading romance.

Chaplin now cuts to a second reverse-angle medium close-up of the flower girl, who picks up a rose, and offers it to him. Back to a medium shot of the tramp, and we see the flower girl from over her shoulder miming, pointing to him, then to the rose, inviting him to enter the store. When he doesn't respond immediately, we go to the third set of shot/reverse shots. In another medium close-up, the flower girl, still holding the rose in her right hand, turns and asks her assistant to go to the cash register. She gets a 50-cent piece and turns back to the tramp, holding the flower in her right hand and coin in the left, in one gesture crystallising the film's primary contrast between the world of romance and the world of money – and the values associated with both. Which world – the erratic, inauthentic world of the millionaire or the kind, supportive world of the blind flower girl – will determine the fates of these two people?

The flower girl offers the tramp both a rose and a coin

When we cut back to the medium shot of the tramp, his smile has faded slightly, and as the flower girl begins to stand, his face conveys a look of apprehension, shyness, perhaps even fear. He turns, apparently about to scurry away from the store. Chaplin matches action, cutting to a medium long shot outside the floral shop, the camera dollying left as the tramp hurries past the door and the flower girl steps outside, beckoning him to return. From the time the flower girl holds up the coin inside the store until she extends the rose toward the tramp, the solo violin and harp have been playing on the soundtrack. As they face one another outside the store, there is another brief rest, and, as she offers him the rose, a second violin plays in harmony with the first. The tramp smiles, turns back toward the flower girl, and reaches his left hand toward her. The two violins and harp continue as the tramp – still separated in space from the flower girl – holds the rose in both hands. Determined to help the poor tramp, the flower girl steps toward him and takes his left hand into her right. As she places the coin into his hand with her left hand, then encircles his hand with both of hers, Chaplin cuts to a medium shot of both, the violin recitative halts, and the film's brilliant finale ensues.

On the one hand, the visual style of this final 58 seconds seems relatively simple: it's essentially (though not exactly) two different

Unaware of the tramp's identity, the flower girl offers him a rose

camera setups – one of the flower girl on the right over the tramp's shoulder, the other of the tramp on the left of the frame with the back of the flower girl in right foreground – and a third transition shot (shot 2, below), all presented in ten shots and three title cards.

1. Medium close-up (MCU) of FG over tramp's shoulder (19 ft, 12 frames)[79]
2. Close-up (CU) of FG's hands holding tramp's left hand – pan left and tilt up as FG's right hand goes up tramp's arm to his coat lapel. Ends with CU of tramp's face and right hand holding flower (13/12)
3. MCU of FG, same as 1 (6/4)
4. Title card: 'You?' (2/14)
5. CU of tramp: raises eyebrows, assents (3/9)
6. MCU of FG, same angle as 1 and 3 but slightly tighter: FG raises right hand to side of face, then places it on her chest (5/14)
7. CU of tramp, same as 5: tramp gestures right index finger toward his eye (3/4)
8. Title card: 'You can see now?' (3/9)
9. CU of tramp, continuation of shot 7: tramp brings right index finger back down (2/10)
10. MCU of FG, continuation of 6: FG moves right hand from chest to top of tramp's hand (7/5)
11. Title card: 'Yes, I can see now.' (4/5)
12. MCU of FG, continuation of 10: FG, tears in eyes, raises her hands and the tramp's left hand to her chest (14/11)
13. CU of tramp, somewhat tighter and slightly right of 9: tramp smiles, still holding rose with right thumb on his lower lip (8/4)

Despite the apparent simplicity, however, it's a brilliant combination of late silent era and early sound era cinema – the climactic moment in this transitional film – drawing especially on the interplay of camera distance and editing, acting style, lighting, and the emotive power of music to help intensify the final moments of the narrative.

One striking feature of these shots is the tight camera distance. Chaplin once told an interviewer that 'the fact is, I've never liked the close-up too much, except for very important moments of emphasis and intimacy'.[80] This is certainly true of *City Lights*, for the film uses close-ups and medium close-ups very sparingly; in many scenes the camera never gets closer than a medium shot to the performers, from the waist up. Yet Chaplin did know that because of the expressiveness of the human face, scenes of emotional power required tight camera distance, and he also knew that cutting between the responses of two different faces using conventional shot/reverse-shot editing could convey complex emotional states. That surely happens here. After the medium long shot of the flower girl handing the rose to the tramp, Chaplin uses only medium close-ups and close-ups, systematically alternating between the flower girl and the tramp. Because the movements of the flower girl's hands are important to the scene, the shots of her face employ a slightly longer camera distance than the shots of the tramp. However, in shot 6, as the emotional pitch heightens, Chaplin frames the flower girl slightly more tightly for the rest of the scene. The tramp, in turn, is framed even more tightly than the flower girl throughout the scene: from the end of shot 2 onward, his right hand stays relatively motionless holding the rose, with his thumb near his mouth. Chaplin the director even moves the camera slightly closer to the tramp in the final shot of the film (see cover illustration) and also swings the camera slightly to the right of the previous framings of the tramp, giving viewers less profile and a slightly more frontal view of his response. And that shot is heartbreaking.

The subtle interplay of the music, acting style, and lighting are also crucial to the effect of the ending. Timothy Brock observes that although some have argued that the music in the final scene is derivative of Puccini, it could only have been written by Chaplin, who was a violinist himself and especially skilled at composing music for strings.[81] The last phase of the music begins in the middle of shot 1 after four beats of rest when the flower girl grasps the tramp's left hand. As Virginia Cherrill's face begins to register recognition of the tramp's identity in the longest take of the sequence, four violins begin

In shot 1 the flower girl shows the first hint of recognition when she touches the tramp's hand

to play: two play an octave apart while the other two play the middle intervals. Significantly, Chaplin had used this same musical motif at two crucial points earlier in the film: he introduced it in the opening medley accompanying the title cards, then returned to it when the tramp gently grasps and kisses the flower girl's hand on the stairway in the courtyard after he's driven her home in the millionaire's car in segment 2c. The four violins continue through the delicate second shot that begins with a close-up of the hands and ends in the close-up

In the delicate moving camera shot 2, cameraman Rollie Totheroh begins with a closeup of the flower girl grasping the tramp's hand, then tilts up and pans left …

... following her hand as she moves up the tramp's arm to touch the same lapel where she pinned a carnation in their first meeting

of the tramp with the flower girl's hand on his lapel, and the reverse shot of the flower girl's reaction, up to the 'You' title card.

When the tramp nods his assent in shot 5 and a solo viola joins the violins, beginning to broaden the chord, his expression contains a touch of apprehension. The burden then shifts to the flower girl as Chaplin cuts to shot 6: her shock that the tramp's identity is so different from the wealthy man she imagined is registered as she places her right hand first at the side of her face, then on her chest.

In shot 6, the flower girl's right hand gestures – to side of face, then to chest – convey her shock and attempt to cope with the startling revelation

Note that the framing is tighter than in shots 1 and 3, and that the backlighting helps frame her head, while the lighting from front left allows us to absorb the complex set of emotions expressed on her face as she begins to process the shock she has just experienced.

Yet the music and emotion continue to build. When the 'You can see now?' card appears, the cellos enter to join the other strings. The title itself adds another layer of complexity: the tramp has asked if her sight has been restored, but as viewers we also wonder if she has gained, or will gain, insight – will see – as she decides how to respond to this stunning news. Cherrill's performance is complex and subtle. In shot 10 she moves her right hand from her chest to the top of the tramp's left hand, and the final title card appears: 'Yes, I can see now.' Here, too, Chaplin chose his words with sublime ambiguity: the flower girl has regained her sight, but we can also interpret her words to mean, 'now I understand'. The same take as shot 10 continues in shot 12 – the second longest take in the scene – but Cherrill's shifting expressions and hand movements remain complex. Her face seems first to express gratitude, but then as she pulls the tramp's hand nearer to her heart, she breathes in and seems close to tears, then returns to a near expression of gratitude just as Chaplin cuts to the final close-up of the tramp.[82]

Lighting, acting, and music then ratchet up the emotional pitch yet one more time. Having rested for twenty-five measures in slow tempo since the flower girl offered the tramp a rose, the basses re-enter, joining the violins, violas, and cellos. The final close-up is lit more brightly than the previous few shots of the tramp: note how brightly the light shines on the right side of his face and how distinctively his eyes glisten (see cover image). Just as the film begins to fade out, the tramp's mouth moves closer to a smile. At this point, the strings display their widest array of colour and sound. A fifteen-note divisi ranges from a high E-flat in the violins, four above middle C, to a mid-range G in the basses, two below middle C.

Throughout the whole final movement, from the moment the

The flower girl's final shot (12) registers a complex range of emotions, from gratitude to near tears as she brings the tramp's hand closer to her heart

flower girl touched the tramp's hand and began to recognise who he is, the music has built, becoming fuller and heavier, as she wrestles with the burden of how to respond to her new insight. The tramp's final expression conveys his joy at seeing the flower girl again and at learning that her sight has been restored, but the hand at the mouth tempers that joy with anxiety and apprehension, leaving us uncertain about their future, even though the flower girl has given him both a fresh rose and a large shiny coin.

The music, too, tempers the joy. As the final close-up of the tramp fades to black, Chaplin makes an unusual musical choice: he begins a long crescendo, climaxing more than 20 seconds after the screen has gone black following 'The End' title card. The winds and brass subtly enter and modulate the final bars of the score, ending in a powerful orchestral tutti in A minor, a striking shift from the high strings that dominated the start of this final movement. We're left with a black screen and a precarious open ending, uncertain of what the fates will bring the flower girl and the tramp. Her gesture of bringing the tramp's hand to her heart and the broadening of the tramp's smile at the end of the final shot can lead an optimist to hope their relationship may flower. Our knowledge of the flower girl's expectation of a rich and kind benefactor, of the tramp's social marginality, and the darker emotional tone of the score's final strains suggest to the pessimist – or even the realist – that this relationship will never work. But Chaplin leaves us poised on the edge, without a definitive answer. As Agee would have it, our hearts have shrivelled. By blending the best of silent era pantomime with the emerging power of a recorded musical score, Chaplin orchestrated a climax of emotional power and complexity richer than he had ever achieved, or ever would again.

But *City Lights* is not designed simply to evoke emotion: it also conveys meaning. I wrote earlier that the film is Chaplin's farewell to the 1920s, and I think that is borne out by the depiction of the millionaire and his world. Chaplin himself knew about the nightlife of the big city in the 1920s, not least in the eight months he spent in New York waiting for his divorce to be settled between January and August 1927. Even though *City Lights* was released as the Great Depression was beginning to bite, the millionaire does not much resemble the stereotypic plutocrat that became a staple villain in the films and literature of the 1930s, like Jim Taylor in Capra's *Mr Smith Goes to Washington* (1939). The factory owner in *Modern Time*s is much more characteristic of that depiction of wealth. Rather, Chaplin uses the millionaire in part to indict the shallowness of the leisured class as it wasted away in the Jazz Age. In that sense it is closer to Fitzgerald's 'Babylon Revisited' (1931) than to Dos Passos's *The Big Money*. Through the cumulative representation of the millionaire's world and moral universe in *City Lights*, Chaplin shows, in Molyneaux's words, that 'the idolatry of business prosperity and big city amusement are humanly counter-productive'.[83]

Through the depiction of the flower girl's world and her touching relationship with the tramp, Chaplin offers the alternative possibility of loving, sacrificing, even mutually sustaining relationships. The tramp's self-sacrifice for the flower girl was doubtless fuelled, even if unconsciously, by Chaplin's desire to help his afflicted mother, a motif that would return even more directly in the relationship between Chaplin's character and the paralysed dancer in *Limelight*. In the love between the flower girl and the tramp, Chaplin also offered a vision of a lasting, loving relationship that had eluded him in his own life but that he would soon approach with Paulette Goddard and later, even more successfully, with Oona O'Neill. In this farewell to the 1920s Chaplin leaves viewers poised between the two central images in the film – the flower and the coin – and invites us to choose between them.

17 Release and Reception

A transitional film poised aesthetically between the late silent and early sound era, *City Lights* was also poised economically between the prosperity of the Jazz Age and the economic distress of the Great Depression. Chaplin premiered his film after the American economy had significantly stalled but before the Depression had hit the movie industry with full force. Clearly, the American economy was declining: total US corporate profits had plummeted from $8.6 billion in 1929 to $2.9 billion in 1930, while in 1931 corporations cumulatively experienced a loss of $900 million. Yet movie industry revenues held relatively steady between 1929 and 1931 at around $720 to $730 million (they would decline to $530 million in 1932). Total profits of the movie companies, however, dropped from $54.5

CHARLES CHAPLIN FILM CORPORATION

NEGATIVE COST OF "CITY LIGHTS"

	Cash cost to December 31 1930	Subsequent adjustment to August 31 1931	Cash cost to August 31, 1931
Publicity	$ 31,238.87	$ 1,678.53	$ 32,917.40
Technical department	16,997.08		16,997.08
Wardrobe department	4,338.58		4,338.58
Stores department	20,629.51	387.89	21,017.40
Regular talent	790,263.84	26,250.00	816,513.84
Extra talent	44,805.17		44,805.17
Scenario	36,325.00		36,325.00
Laboratory	51,014.73	20,056.49	71,071.22
Electrical department	42,700.96	376.39	43,077.35
Camera department	50,986.29	1,437.00	52,423.29
Carpenter department	72,838.59	628.20	73,464.79
Music	1,815.17	37,062.75	38,877.92
Studio rent	160,000.00	5,000.00	165,000.00
Light and heat	8,064.04	314.07	8,378.11
Telephone and telegraph	4,795.38	208.89	5,002.27
Postage	710.00	15.00	725.00
Water	2,136.75	39.69	2,176.44
Insurance - negative	13,440.00		13,440.00
Insurance - liability	6,702.62	88.51	6,721.33
Auto expense	12,872.56	255.94	13,128.50
Miscellaneous	11,872.62	176.19	12,048.81
Properties purchased	3,595.37		3,595.37
Properties rented	7,416.72		7,416.72
Wardrobe purchased	1,397.13		1,397.13
Wardrobe rented	690.98		690.98
Negative raw stock	36,421.34		36,421.34
Positive raw stock	5,817.00		5,817.00
Paint and wall paper	24,502.13		24,494.02
	$1,474,392.43	$93,961.43	$1,558,353.84

These figures compiled by Price, Waterhouse and Company.

The *City Lights* budget was about four times the average budget for a Hollywood feature film in 1930, not surprising, given the length of the production million in 1929 to $52 million in 1930 to only $3.4 million in 1931; in 1932 the movie companies would *lose* $55.7 million.[84] Given this deteriorating situation in the American economy, with the movie industry sliding in the same direction, and given the financial pressures placed on Chaplin before he started the film, how did *City Lights* fare at the box office and with the critics?

I might begin answering that question by asking how much the film cost. Not surprisingly, given its long production schedule, *City Lights* was an expensive film for its day. The average budget for a Hollywood feature film in 1930 was $375,000. Once all production costs were calculated, including the expenses for the musical score, *City Lights* cost over $1,568,000, about four times the average Hollywood budget.

During January 1931, Chaplin and his collaborators worked feverishly to get the film ready for a 30 January Los Angeles premiere, completing recording sessions at 2 a.m. on 7 January, preparing a preview print, and working on publicity. After previewing the film at the Tower Theater in Los Angeles on 19 January 1931, Chaplin tightened the editing, then had Alfred Newman and the orchestra re-record some of the music to fit the new cut.

It's hard to appreciate how much excitement the Los Angeles premiere generated at this high point in the director's career. Perhaps the best contemporary parallel is the enthusiasm that accompanied the release of each new *Star Wars* film, once the series had become ingrained in the American cultural imagination. Chaplin's towering reputation, combined with the oddity of releasing a non-dialogue film long after the talkies had arrived, helped fuel the excitement. For the site of the premiere, Chaplin chose a brand-new movie palace, the Los Angeles Theater. The day before the 30 January premiere – of both the theatre and the film – the *Los Angeles Express* carried a feature article on the theatre, trumpeting its 2,200 seats, its spacious layout (no more than six seats in a row between aisles), its café and soda fountain, its crying room (with a miniature screen and earphones for mothers tending babies), and its art gallery with exhibits changing monthly.[85]

On 29 January 1931, the day before the release of City Lights, the Los Angeles Express carried a feature article about the brand-new Los Angeles Theater and included this sketch of the elegant movie palace

The premiere itself was a huge event: the 2,200 seats had been sold out at $10 a ticket for over ten days: studios and individuals had bought large blocks of tickets. Pandemonium reigned outside the theatre. The UPI reported that 400 policemen kept a crowd of 50,000 people in order (others estimated half that many), as the onlookers stretched necks to see their favourites exit limousines and parade into the theatre. Scientist Albert Einstein and his wife accompanied Chaplin. Hollywood luminaries like producers David Selznick, Carl Laemmle Sr and Jr, and Jack Warner; directors Joseph von Sternberg, Norman McLeod, and Clarence Brown; stars Gloria Swanson, Gary Cooper, and Mary Pickford; screenwriters Herman Mankiewicz and Jules Furthman; and moguls William Randolph Hearst and Howard Hughes joined in the festivities. Louella Parsons gushed, 'What an opening! Dazzling lights, gorgeously gowned women wearing their best bibs and tuckers and a theater that is the last word in comfort and beauty. All this made Charlie's entrance cue for "City Lights" perfectly timed.' It was, added the UPI reporter, 'one of Los Angeles' most spectacular premieres'.[86]

Chaplin left the next day for New York, where a premiere at the George M. Cohan Theater was also highly anticipated. Mordaunt Hall at the New York Times had run stories about City Lights as early as July and August 1929, and Chaplin arranged to have his article, 'Pantomime and Comedy', a defence of the universal art of pantomime films, run in the *Times* on 31 January. Even though the Cohan wasn't the top Manhattan movie palace – it was originally built for live performances in 1911 – the premiere, on 6 February, kicked off a tremendous twelve-week run, garnering over $450,000 in ticket sales. Of the opening, columnist Walter Winchell wrote: 'What a grand satisfaction it must have been to Chaplin to sit among his critics and hear them join in the Bravos!'[87]

The New York premiere concluded, Chaplin set sail on 13 February for England aboard the *Mauritania* with his valet Kono and Ralph Barton. The trip began a sixteen-month world tour, but Chaplin's first task was to attend the London premiere of *City Lights* at the Dominion Theatre on 27 February. From the moment the comedian set foot on British shores, the press chronicled Chaplin's every move – from meeting with prominent politicians to visiting the Hanwell School where he was placed as a youth when his mother was hospitalised.[88] Like the Los Angeles premiere, those attending had to make their way through large crowds to get to the Dominion.

Chaplin speaks with George Bernard Shaw at the London Premiere of *City Lights*, first row balcony at the Dominion Theatre. Ralph Barton is in the foreground

Chaplin's party, which included Ralph Barton, George Bernard Shaw, and Lord and Lady Astor, sat prominently in the dress circle. The British paper *The Daily Herald* reported that the start of the film was held up for fifteen minutes by sustained applause. After the screening, a deeply moved Chaplin stepped briefly before the adoring audience to convey his thanks: 'It is silly for me to try to express myself here. You understand how I feel and your affection and your appreciation makes me proud to be in my own country.' Shaw responded after the screening: 'In all my life, I have never before known what comedy truly meant. . . . The little fellow is a genius whom none of us has properly appreciated.' The next day Chaplin said that getting such a warm reception in his native country 'was one of the greatest emotional experiences of my life'.[89] The three premieres kicked off both the film and Chaplin's world tour. He would later attend equally enthusiastic premieres in Berlin and Paris.

How well did the film do at the box office? This is a difficult and complicated question because of Chaplin's unique status in the film industry. He paid for his own production costs through his studio, the Charles Chaplin Film Corporation, but he released his films through United Artists, a company he co-owned, and his studio had an arrangement with United Artists to get a certain percentage of the revenues that UA received from exhibitors for the rights to show his films. According to a 27 December 1930 letter from Arthur Kelly of United Artists, Chaplin's studio received 75 per cent of all revenues his films earned in the United States; 70 per cent of revenues in Canada, Alaska, and the British Isles; 60 per cent of revenues in Germany, Australia, the Far East, and Mexico; and 50 per cent of those in South America and Continental Europe, excluding Germany.[90] United Artists retained the remainder. With that in mind, the United Artists balance sheet at the end of 1931 shows that *City Lights* had already brought in $1,947,899.76 to the company.[91] From that total, Chaplin's studio received its percentage, depending on the source of the revenue. However, because contracts for international distribution were still being made in 1932, we must look forward. In a letter of 12

June 1934 to Sydney Chaplin, Chaplin's business manager Alf Reeves wrote that 'the net amount of money received by the [Charles Chaplin Film] corporation on "City Lights" since its release in January 1931 is $3,006,308.74'. Reeves added that $1.638,355.60 of that came from outside the US and Canada.[92] Because the film was still playing in Japan, the final total was probably a bit higher, but it's fair to generalise that even in the declining economic times (times which became much worse in 1932), *City Lights* earned Chaplin's studio twice what it cost him to make. From that standpoint, Chaplin's decision to resist the talkies was a resounding success.

What about the critical response? Two large clippings albums in the Archives de Montreux testify to how positive the response was to Chaplin and the film: Album 33, which contains the US press response, and Album 34, with the British response, are filled with articles, reviews, and editorials about Chaplin and *City Lights*. A survey of all that material suggests that in general, the film received widespread attention and glowing reviews in both the United States and England, not only from the trade press and newspapers but also from more highbrow publications.

Two examples of the most extravagant praise appeared in *New Republic* and the *New Statesman and Nation*. In the former, Gilbert Seldes – an early advocate of taking the popular arts seriously and a Chaplin enthusiast – could hardly restrain himself. Titling his review 'A Comic Masterpiece', Seldes wrote,

The immediate effect of the picture is that it is funnier than many things he has done and infinitely inventive; the second effect is that it is magnificently organized, deeply thought out and felt, and communicated with an unflagging energy and a masterly technique. Chaplin is the only artist whose pictures always give the impression of having been created before your eyes, with the extraordinary result that when you see them you cannot believe they have been shown before and that when you see them a second time, you are constantly surprised and elated by their perfection.[93]

If anything, the *New Statesman and Nation* reached for even higher plaudits:

Mr Chaplin can neither be praised nor blamed in comparison with anyone else. He is the only great artist the film has produced; his taste is as discreet as it is spontaneous, his morality is as sublime as it is simple. He is at once the most tragic and most comic figure of the day. There is nothing he cannot do, no emotion he cannot suggest; so there is no limit to his sympathetic understanding of life. Hence it is almost impossible to say anything about him.

Searching for *something* to criticise, the reviewer felt that the plot was episodic and lacked unity but then recovered to say that the film should thus be regarded as 'a succession of brilliant episodes'.[94] Both reviews suggest that Chaplin had succeeded, beyond even his expectations, with his comedy romance in pantomime.

Of course, not all commentary was so purely positive. *Variety*, for example, while praising the film and predicting 'heavy b.o. receipts', hedged that 'there is some doubt about its holdover power'.[95] But on the whole, the reviewers treated Chaplin with high regard, even reverence, and greeted the film with accolades.[96] In fact, the release of *City Lights* even prompted editorial writers and columnists who rarely wrote about movies to weigh in on Chaplin's achievements as a film-maker, artist, and commentator on art and society. In particular, his defence of pantomime and his assault on the talkies generated debate about a possible return to pantomime, but the consensus seemed to be that Chaplin was really in a class by himself: he might continue to make engaging and memorable movies without dialogue, but the industry would not take the road now less travelled back to the silent era. His special niche as pantomimic genius firmly carved out, his new film a hit with the press and the public, Chaplin had hit the bull's-eye. As he began to tour the world, he was on top of it.

18 The Legacy of City Lights

City Lights and Chaplin's world tour following its premiere ushered in a socio-aesthetic shift in Chaplin's career as a film-maker, yet the film has lived on in interesting ways since that time. One of the few negative reviews of *City Lights*, Alexander Bakshy's 'Charlie Chaplin Falters', appeared in the *Nation*. Countering the 'fervent acclaim' the film had elicited, Bakshy judged it 'the feeblest of his longer pictures', because 'Chaplin's growing seriousness, his desire to be more than a mere comedian', embedded in the romantic plot, has mistakenly 'deceived him into holding sentiment more precious than fun'.[97]

Bakshy's observation about Chaplin's growing sense of seriousness was prescient: one of the by-products of the attention he was garnering was that his opinions about current affairs were being solicited, and, unlike his films, Chaplin was starting to talk. Increasingly, he responded to interviewers with comments like 'Something is wrong – things have been badly managed when five million men are out of work in the richest nation in the world. . . . It seems to me that the question is not whether the country is wet or dry but whether the country is starved or fed.' In this case his remarks led the interviewer to comment, 'Consciously a millionaire, subconsciously his funny feet are reaching for a soapbox.'[98] As he toured the world in 1931–2, observing deteriorating economic conditions and talking with reporters and world leaders about the problems of the day, Chaplin turned more toward commentary on world affairs.

Upon his return to the US in the depths of the Depression, Chaplin found that critics like Harry Alan Potamkin and Lorenzo Turrent Rozas were criticising the 'maudlin pathos' in his films and calling for a more politically progressive art.[99] That in turn led to three feature films which engaged more directly with current social concerns than at any other time in Chaplin's career: *Modern Times*, in which the tramp tries to make ends meet as a factory worker during the instability of the Depression; *The Great Dictator* (1940), Chaplin's frontal satiric assault on Hitler and fascism; and *Monsieur Verdoux* (1947), about a dapper French bank teller who, thrown out of work during the Depression after thirty years on the job, becomes a Bluebeard, marrying and then murdering rich widows to support his family. The first two of these films, particularly the second, received widespread acclaim. However, the third, released early in the Cold War, was a box-office disaster in the United States, boycotted by conservative veterans groups who considered Chaplin a dangerous leftist because of several speeches he made in 1942 praising the fighting spirit of our Russian allies and calling for the opening of a second front in World War Two.[100] By the late 1940s, Chaplin's public reputation in the US was as low as it had ever been since he first ascended to stardom in 1915.

Following the failure of *Monsieur Verdoux* in the US, Chaplin decided by the end of that decade to back away from commenting publicly on political concerns and instead to set about repairing his faded star image. Aptly, he returned to *City Lights* as a part of that effort. In 1950 United Artists helped Chaplin engineer a re-release of the film, in part by preparing a new press book which included ads that featured the beloved tramp character. The ad also resurrected a 1931 quotation from Walter Winchell, in which the gossip columnist praised Chaplin and the movie after attending the New York premiere at the Cohan. Although the re-release of the film did not convert all of Chaplin's conservative detractors, it did return the tramp to the cultural conversation and pleased old fans and new initiates. Re-released at a time when the American movie industry was struggling, *City Lights* received an unexpected recognition: *Life* magazine named it the best film of 1950.

Since that time, *City Lights* has held a central position in Chaplin's canon: when he decided to re-release a number of his feature films for extended runs at the Plaza Theater in Manhattan in late 1963 and 1964, *City Lights* was the first film that played and,

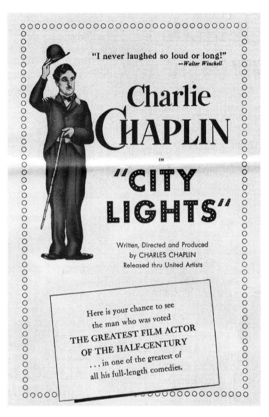

This advertisement from the 1950 City Lights press book quoted from a 1931 Walter Winchell column about the New York premiere of the film

with *Monsieur Verdoux*, enjoyed the longest run (nine weeks each). When Chaplin decided to make his films available again in 1971 and 1972 – partly in connection with his 1972 return to the United States to receive an honorary Academy Award – *City Lights* was a key film in that series. As home video became an option, the film was made available first on VHS, then on laserdisc, and finally on DVD. We have every reason to expect, as new home video formats emerge, that *City Lights* will be released on those as well.

What of its current reputation in Chaplin's body of work and in film history generally? Among admirers of his work, some prefer the

more anarchic comic inventiveness of the early Keystone to Mutual period, others his more sustained narratives that blend silent film comedy with pathos, while some prefer the later and more politically engaged Chaplin. For the first group, *City Lights* contains wonderful scenes, like the boxing-match sequence, both in the locker room and in the ring, and small but inspired moments, as when the tramp, wearing a tuxedo, jumps out of the car and wrests a cigar butt away from a bum, or when he defiantly and resiliently kicks his cigarette butt after tossing it over his shoulder as he's being led into jail. For the last group, more engaged with Chaplin the politically informed artist, *City Lights* is less inspired, too sweet, a film that only foreshadows his most important work in movies like *Modern Times*, *The Great Dictator*, and even *Monsieur Verdoux*. For most of those in the middle group, though, *City Lights* represents the full and most successful flowering of the unique blend of comedy, romance, and pathos that Chaplin had been experimenting with at least since *The Tramp* and *The Bank* in 1915.

In the longer lens of film history *City Lights* must be considered one of the culminating masterpieces of silent film comedy, the film genre from the silent era that has probably survived most successfully into our new millennium, even as the film makes skilful use of the new sound technology. To my mind, Chaplin was working at his peak, although in somewhat different modes, in the two films at the exact centre of his eight United Artists features. *Modern Times*, the fifth United Artists feature, showed Chaplin moving into his more overtly political art with a penetrating comic vision. In *City Lights*, the fourth, Chaplin deftly created a story of moral weight and thematic resonance which draws effectively on brilliant pantomime and a recorded musical score to evoke both laughter and pathos. It's a crowning achievement, and it still breaks our hearts.

Notes

Abbreviations:
CA: Chaplin Archives, Cineteca di Bologna, Italy (Chaplin Production Records)
AdM: Archives de Montreux, Switzerland (Chaplin Clippings Albums)

1 I will refer to the character Chaplin plays in *City Lights* as 'the tramp'. Chaplin's comic persona in his movies is not always accurately called a tramp, and he's sometimes been referred to as 'Charlie'. As he's most often called 'the tramp' in the script versions of *City Lights,* that's the name I will use.
2 This essay originally appeared in the 3 September 1949 issue of *Life*. I'm quoting from James Agee, *Film Writing and Selected Journalism* (New York: The Library of America, 2005), p. 19.
3 Richard Meryman, 'Ageless Master's Anatomy of Comedy: Chaplin, an Interview', in Kevin H. Hayes (ed.) *Charlie Chaplin: Interviews* (Jackson: University of Mississippi Press, 2005), p. 134. Chaplin's memory seems to be good. The daily production reports from the film indicate that he took seven takes (nos. 4328–34) at the end of the day on 22 September 1930, ultimately using the final take in the film. More later on the daily production reports.
4 Charles Chaplin interviewed by Peter Bogdanovich, 8 February 1973. Thanks to Jeffrey Vance for calling my attention to this interview. This confirms what Chaplin told Richard Meryman in a 1966 interview. Asked if he had a favourite, Chaplin chose *City Lights*. Selections from the Meryman interview are reprinted in Jeffrey Vance, *Chaplin:*

Genius of the Cinema (New York: Harry N. Abrams, 2003), pp. 360–7, with the *City Lights* quotation on p. 367.
5 David Robinson, *Chaplin: His Life and Art* (New York: McGraw-Hill, 1985), p. 103. Robinson's outstanding biography, the first written by a film historian who had access to Chaplin's private papers and records, is the starting point for any reader or scholar interested in Chaplin. Like all scholars of Chaplin, I am indebted to his work. Another valuable biography is Vance's *Chaplin: Genius of the Cinema*. Besides providing a well-researched overview of Chaplin's career, the book makes marvellous use of photographs from Chaplin's holdings. Kenneth Lynn's *Charlie Chaplin and His Times* (New York: Simon and Schuster, 1997) provides interesting additional contextual information about Chaplin's early years but is generally hostile to his more politically engaged work and involvements from *Modern Times* onward.
6 Charles J. McGuirk, 'Chaplinitis', *Motion Picture Magazine*, vol. 9 nos 6–7, July–August 1915), pp. 85–9, 121–4.
7 The inflation calculator, provided by the US Bureau of Labor Statistics, is available online at <data.bls.gov/cgi-bin/cpicalc.pl>
8 Vance gives a good account of the agreement with First National in *Genius*, p. 85.
9 Ibid., p. 85.
10 At two points Chaplin uses on-location footage: when the millionaire and the tramp drive home after their night at the cabaret (shot at several locations in Los Angeles) and in the shot when the tramp buys all the flower

girl's flowers. In the second case, the scene is cut to look as if that location (a building at the corner of Wilshire Boulevard and Commonwealth Avenue) is adjacent to the millionaire's mansion. For an excellent book on the sets and locations of Chaplin's films, a veritable cinematic archaeology of the Los Angeles area, see John Bengston, *Silent Traces: Discovering Early Hollywood through the Films of Charlie Chaplin* (Santa Monica: Santa Monica Press, 2006).

11 Robert Sherwood, 'Review of *A Woman of Paris*', in Anthony Slide (ed.), *Selected Film Criticism, 1921–1930*, (Metuchen, NJ: Scarecrow Press, 1982), p. 318, and Stark Young, 'Dear Mr Chaplin', *New Republic*, vol. 31, 23 August 1922, p. 358.

12 Charles Chaplin, *My Autobiography* (New York: Simon and Schuster, 1964), p. 326. Subsequently referred to as *MA* in the text.

13 Robinson, *Chaplin*, p. 371. The original divorce complaint, the answer to it, Grey's cross-complaint, and Chaplin's answer to the cross-complaint, along with a number of other court decisions and documents related to the divorce proceedings, are reprinted in Lita Grey Chaplin and Jeffrey Vance, *Wife of the Life of the Party* (Lanham, MD: Scarecrow Press, 1998), pp. 131–297. The quotations come from pp. 133 and 136.

14 'Chaplins at Last Find Divorce Court Path', *Variety* vol. 85, 12 January 1927, p. 4.

15 The court order is reprinted in Chaplin and Vance, *Wife of the Life of the Party*, pp. 287–8.

16 *New York Times*, 16 January 1927, p. 5; 23 January 1927, p. 1; 28 January 1927, p. 7.

17 Harry Crocker, 'Charlie Chaplin: Man and Mime', unpublished manuscript

(Beverly Hills, CA: Margaret Herrick Library, AMPAS, 1953), ch. XII, p. 4.

18 Undated letter (probably late January or early February 1927), Sydney Chaplin to Charlie Chaplin, CA, document 00314781.

19 'Cost Chaplin $2,000,000 in All for Divorce: Many Other Costs Besides Settlement – 1st Divorce Cheaper', *Variety*, vol. 88 no. 7, 31 August 1927, p. 3.

20 The interlocutory judgment is reprinted in Chaplin and Vance, *Wife of the Life of the Party*, pp. 295–7.

21 'Chaplin Settles Tax', *New York Times*, 10 February 1928, p. 26.

22 Sydney Chaplin to Charlie Chaplin, 1 September 1926, CA, document 00008340.

23 Reeves to Sydney Chaplin, CA, document 00008349.

24 The production report files for *City Lights*, CA, document 00313463, run from 21 November 1927, when Chaplin was completing the scoring of *The Circus*, to 14 March 1931, after the London release of *City Lights*. The reports were prepared by Chaplin's Continuity Reporter, Della Steele, and contain a treasure trove of information about the production history of the film. Steele compiled weekly reports through Christmas of 1928, then began with daily production reports on 27 December 1928, when, according to the DPR, 'Opening shots taken for "City Lights"'. Hereafter, rather than footnoting each reference to this document, I will refer to these documents in the text either as WPR (weekly production report) or DPR (daily production report), followed by the date.

25 Robinson, *Chaplin*, pp. 51–7.

26 Vance, *Chaplin*, p. 194.

27 Reeves to Sydney Chaplin, 27 August 1928, CA, document 00008498.

28 Crocker, 'Charlie Chaplin', ch. XII, pp. 8–9.

29 Reeves to Sydney Chaplin, CA, document 00008498; Charlie Chaplin to Sydney Chaplin, CA, document 8497; Reeves to Sydney Chaplin, 31 August 1927, CA, document 0008495.

30 Donald Crafton, *The Talkies: American Cinema's Transition to Sound, 1926–1931* (New York: Charles Scribner's Sons, 1997), pp. 76–87, 108–11, 15.

31 'Movie Stars Give Big Radio Program', *New York Times*, 30 March 1928, p. 30.

32 *Variety*, 4 April 1928, p. 9.

33 *Film Daily*, 2 July 1928, p. 3.

34 Reeves to Sydney Chaplin, 29 January 1929, CA, document 00008427.

35 Gladys Hall, 'Charlie Chaplin Attacks the Talkies', *Motion Picture Magazine,* vol. 37, May 1929, p. 29.

36 Quoted in Robinson, *Chaplin*, p. 401.

37 'Production record, *City Lights*', CA, document 00004903.

38 In co-operation with the Cineteca di Bologna, I am editing a forthcoming edition of the production history of *City Lights*. This book will contain reproductions of some of the most crucial primary documents that help us detail the story of the making of *City Lights* and the artistic contributions of Chaplin and his collaborators, supplemented by an introduction and commentary on the documents.

39 Crocker, 'Charlie Chaplin', Ch. XI, pp. 15, 14, and 9–16 passim.

40 CA, document 00004685, p. 03411013.

41 Chaplin did shoot the scene but decided not to use it in the final film. Wonderful as a stand-alone comic sequence, it is included in part 3 of

Kevin Brownlow and David Gill's fascinating documentary, *The Unknown Chaplin* (1983).

42 'Continuity of Story', CA, folder 00004689, p. 03412006.

43 'Story Notes as of February 28, 1930', CA, document 00004685, p. 03411024.

44 Information for comparison comes from the following production reports in the CA: *The Circus*, document 00313536; *City Lights*, document 00004903; *Modern Times*, document 00313406; *The Great Dictator*, document 00312495.

45 Alistair Cooke, *Six Men* (New York: Knopf, 1977), p. 36.

46 Not really a socialite from Chicago, as often described, Cherrill was born on a farm near Carthage, Illinois. Her parents separated when she was five, and she did win a scholarship to the fashionable Starrett Finishing School for Girls in Chicago. Cherrill says she was 'discovered' when attending a boxing match at the Hollywood Legion Stadium. Near-sighted, she refused to wear glasses, and a man in tennis clothes whom she didn't recognise (Chaplin) asked her if she would like to be in movies. Many were tested for the role, and when the twenty-year-old was offered the job and told Chaplin she had no experience, he replied, 'That's what I want, otherwise you would have to unlearn what you know, as I do things differently. I will show you what to do.' Production stills and stories from the set confirm that's just what Chaplin did. Virginia Cherrill Martini, in interviews with Jeffrey Vance, 1995–6.

47 Master Shooting List and Notations, CA, document 00313458.

48 Egon Erwin Kisch, compiled by Harold B. Segel, 'Working with Charlie

Chaplin', in *Egon Erwin Kisch, the Raging Reporter: A Bio-Anthology* (West Lafayette, IN: Purdue University Press, 1997), pp. 248–60.

49 Chaplin, MA, p. 326.

50 It would be ten years before Crocker would work for Chaplin again, this time as a publicist.

51 Virginia Cherrill Martini interviews with Jeffrey Vance, 1995–6.

52 DPR, 11 November 1929, CA, document 00313463, and Master Shooting List and Notations, CA, document 00313458, p. 118.

53 Seven minutes of those screen tests are included on disk 2 of the MK2 City Lights DVD (Warner Bros. 37648).

54 Cherrill interview with Vance, quoted in Vance, *Chaplin*, p. 204.

55 As I use the term, the artist may not be conscious of 'submerged autobiography'. I would speculate that by creating characters that seem authentic and convincing, artists often draw on different parts of their own personalities that they know to be true by their personal experience. The flower girl's world, which resembles the Victorian world of Chaplin's childhood, and the millionaire's world, one similar to the one he knew in the 1920s, are more vivid and convincing because Chaplin knew them both.

56 It's interesting that after the release of *City Lights* and his world tour following the film, Chaplin began the first relatively successful and long-term relationship with a woman when he became involved with Paulette Goddard.

57 For an insightful discussion of the ways in which Chaplin's failed and strained relationships affected his psyche and deepened his art in the

1920s, see Constance Brown Kuriyama, 'Chaplin's Impure Comedy: The Art of Survival', *Film Quarterly* vol. 45 no. 3, Spring 1992, pp. 26–38.

58 Lynn, *Charlie Chaplin*, pp. 333–4. Chaplin notes in his autobiography (p. 348) that Barton did eventually commit suicide, shortly after accompanying Chaplin to London during the start of his world tour following the release of *City Lights*, then returning home.

59 In *Film Art* David Bordwell and Kristin Thompson define 'segmentation' as 'the process of dividing a film into parts for analysis'. See David Bordwell and Kristin Thompson, *Film Art: An Introduction*, 6th edn. (New York: McGraw-Hill, 2001), p. 433.

60 Walter Kerr, *The Silent Clowns* (New York: Knopf, 1975), p. 346. Chaplin's music-hall experience with Fred Karno is relevant, for there he observed both comedy and pathos in abundance. His ability to balance both with such effectiveness in *City Lights* stems both from his special genius and from his grounding in the British music halls.

61 That the flower – the central image of romance in the film – generates comedy in this scene affirms Kerr's claim that the comedy and pathos are 'immaculately interlocked' in the narrative. Furthermore, the scene rebuts Chaplin's critics who charge that he wallows in pathos: here it's undercut with consummate timing and skill.

62 Gerald Weales, *Canned Goods as Caviar: American Film Comedy in the 1930s* (Chicago: University of Chicago Press, 1985), p. 11.

63 Interestingly, although *City Lights* encountered no regulatory difficulties with the Studio Relations Committee of the MPPDA, the *City Lights* file contains a letter to Will Hays from one moviegoer, F. R. DeCourcy, who was offended by the use of the national anthem, claiming that while the audience came 'to strict attention', the tramp character 'goes through grotesque antics to its strains'. He called upon Hays to stop playing the film and explain why it was approved by the 'Motion Picture Censors', Letter, DeCourcy to Will Hays, 14 April 1931, *City Lights* File, MPAA Collection, Margaret Herrick Library, Los Angeles.

64 The theatre and tobacco store face east-southeast on the southwest block 2 in the city set. See page 42.

65 As John Bengston notes in his fascinating visual archaeology of the settings of Chaplin's movies, Chaplin changes locations in the city set when he cuts from the exterior to the interior shot, going across the street to block 4. Behind the tramp in this shot is the men's furnishings store, which is one store up from the florist shop in block 1 where the film will end. See the next image, as well as Bengston, *Silent Traces*, p. 257.

66 The longest take in the film is the shot when the millionaire pours liquor down the tramp's pants in scene 1g, which runs 107 seconds. The third longest take, at 80 seconds, starts at the beginning of the second round of the boxing match and ends when Chaplin cuts to a tighter shot of the tramp getting the rope attached to the bell wrapped around his neck.

67 This gentler side becomes more pronounced when the tramp smiles and tries to ingratiate himself to the replacement boxer (Hank Mann) in scene 5c, hoping he will split the

winnings no matter who is the victor. The boxer, misconstruing the tramp's over-enthusiastic attempts to be friendly as a come-on, promptly goes behind a curtain to change his clothes.

68 Padilla, born the same year as Chaplin (1889), was trained at the Madrid Conservatory and in Italy before beginning his song-writing career. 'La Violetera' was a popular song in the US in the 1920s, recorded in a Spanish version by Raquel Meller, and subsequently by a number of other groups. The head of the French company that owned the rights to 'La Violetera' protested when it felt that Padilla was not adequately credited in the film. After some correspondence, Chaplin agreed to let the company publish music from his next film in France in exchange for dropping any further legal action. See Letter, Alf Reeves to Nathan Burkan, 1 September 1932, CA, document 00005476.

'La Violetera' is the only music published before the film that is widely used in the film, although we also hear a few bars from a number of songs, including 'Star Spangled Banner', 'St Louis Blues', 'I Hear You Calling Me', and 'How Dry I Am'.

69 These sets provide another example of Chaplin's ability to suggest a large city in economically efficient ways: the same set was used for the millionaire's living room and his two bedrooms. If you look closely at the two arched windows and surrounding moulding in the living room set above, you'll recognise the same basic set structure (albeit with different camera setups to hide the similarities) in the two bedroom scenes.

70 Although we associate the tramp with his typical costume, in *City Lights* he wears a wide variety of costumes – his regular tramp costume at the start of the film, formal wear when he's partying with the millionaire, a street sweeper's uniform, boxing gloves and trunks during the boxing scene, and an especially threadbare and ragged version of the tramp costume in the film's final scene.

71 Production stills taken on this set indicate that the front of the millionaire's mansion is located on the north side of block 1 in the city set (see page 42). The camera in this shot would then be across the street near block 3, facing south.

72 Weales aptly notes that the tramp is ill-suited to give up his independence for the world of work. By juxtaposing the street-cleaner scenes with the boxing scenes, writes Weales, the tramp learns that if you give up your independence, 'you may end up either shoveling shit or having it knocked out of you'. Indeed, the moment that the tramp is counted out in the boxing match – his hopes to earn the rent money for the flower girl dashed – audiences accustomed to happy endings in romantic comedies often gasp in disbelief. See Weales, *Canned Goods as Caviar*, p. 26.

73 Gerard Molyneaux, *Charles Chaplin's 'City Lights': Its Production and Dialectical Structure* (New York: Garland, 1983), p. 226.

74 Chaplin was fortunate to work with two talented young musicians who were relatively new to movies. Arthur Johnston (1898–1954) was a songwriter and composer who served as a personal pianist and assistant to Irving Berlin,

and as musical director on a number of Berlin's early stage shows. He came to Hollywood in 1930, serving as musical arranger for *City Lights*, then composed many movie scores in the 1930s, including Mae West's *Bell of the Nineties* (1934) and several Bing Crosby vehicles. Among his most famous songs is 'Pennies from Heaven'. Alfred Newman (1901–70) began working in Hollywood as a conductor and musical director in 1930. He soon became a major composer, winning forty-five Academy Award nominations in his career and winning nine, as well as the anchor of a composing family. His brothers Lionel and Emil were composers, as are his sons Thomas and David, his daughter Maria, and his nephew Randy.

75 Timothy Brock, 'The Intimate Score of the Tramp-Composer: Restoring Music for *City Lights*', in *Prima della rivoluzione: il sogno di una cosa* (Bologna: Le Mani, 2004). See <www.timothybrock.com/ articles_city_lights.htm> to access this online. I am indebted to Timothy Brock for discussing the *City Lights* score with me in Bologna in July 2006 and January 2007 and helping me recognise the way the music functions from the perspective of a trained composer.

I will be discussing the Dolby 5.1 digital transfer of the original score on the Mk2 DVD of the film (Warner Bros. 37648). The Image Entertainment DVD of the film (CBS-Fox ID9181CYDVD) contains a mono transfer of the original score and also Carl Davis's 1989 recording, which uses a larger orchestra.

76 Gerald Mast points out that 'for those who like Christian symbolism', the millionaire denies the tramp three times – this one the third – paralleling

Peter's three denials of Christ following the crucifixion. Gerald Mast, *The Comic Mind: Comedy and the Movies*, 2nd edn. (Chicago: University of Chicago Press, 1979), p. 108.

77 The pea-shooter in the scene was played by Robert Parrish, who later became a Hollywood editor (winning an Academy Award for *Body and Soul* in 1947) and director. He has written briefly about Chaplin's directing style in Robert Parrish, 'An Article on Charlie Chaplin' (1989), CA, document 00004680.

78 By this I mean that the harp provides the chord structure from which the solo violin carries out his tune, all the way up to the moment when the flower girl places the money in the tramp's hand and we have another pause, leading into the final musical passage.

79 Shot lengths taken from *City Lights* Cutting Continuity, CA, document 00313454. One foot of 35mm film consists of sixteen frames. At twenty-four frames per second, a foot of film takes 0.667 seconds to project. A 19ft, twelve-frame shot thus takes about 13 seconds. Subsequent shot lengths are listed in feet and frames, separated by a slash.

80 Meryman, 'Ageless Master's Anatomy of Comedy', p. 133.

81 Brock points to two other good examples of Chaplin's use of strings in his scores: the theme in *Modern Times* that later became known as 'Smile' and the burning of the ghetto scene in *The Great Dictator*. Brock told me that when he conducts Chaplin's scores, the string players, trained for years in the most modern techniques in orchestral playing, often initially consider some of his string passages unusual; and they

are, says Brock, unique to Chaplin's self-taught style. However, once the violinists get accustomed to the 1920s style of playing – e.g. sliding between notes and playing with heavy vibrato – and to Chaplin's own peculiar style of violin playing, they find these string passages very beautiful. Interview, Bologna, Italy, 5 July 2006.

82 Cherrill's complexly shifting facial expressions in this shot illustrates what Chaplin argued in the article he wrote for the *New York Times* the Sunday before *City Lights* premiered in Los Angeles: 'Action is more generally understood than words. The lift of an eyebrow, however faint, may convey more than a hundred words.' See Charles Chaplin, 'Pantomime and Comedy', *New York Times*, Section VIII, 25 January 1931, p. 6.

83 Molyneaux, *Charles Chaplin's 'City Lights'*, p. 226.

84 Joel Finler, *The Hollywood Story* (New York: Crown, 1988), p. 32.

85 The accounts of the Los Angeles and New York premieres are drawn from newspaper clippings in the Chaplin Clippings Albums, AdM, Album 33.

86 Ronald Wagoner, '50,000 Jam Streets at Premiere of Chaplin Film', *Oakland Tribune*, 31 January 1931; Louella Parsons, '*City Lights*, Chaplin Film, Here: Pantomimic Play Solid Smash at New Theater', *Los Angeles Examiner*, 31 January 1931, p. 4. AdM, Album 33. See also Eleanor Barnes, '*City Lights* is Chaplin Hit: Throngs Jam Downtown', CA, document 03572001.

87 Walter Winchell, 'On Broadway', *Des Moines Tribune-Capitol*, 15 February 1931, AdM, Album 33.

88 Chaplin wrote about his world tour in *A Comedian Sees the World*, published serially by *Women's Home Companion* between September 1933 and January 1934. *Comedian* has just been reissued for the first time in book form, ably edited by Lisa Stein. The project was initiated by Progetto Chaplin at the Cineteca di Bologna. See Charles Chaplin, in Lisa Stein (ed.), *A Comedian Sees the World/Il comico vede il mondo* (Genoa: Le Mani, 2006).

89 'Charlie's Thanks in His Maiden Speech', *Daily Herald*, 28 February 1931, and 'Mr Chaplin on *City Lights*', *The Observer*, 1 March 1931, AdM, Album 34.

90 Arthur Kelly, letter, 27 December (Cineteca di Bologna, 1930), p. 1.

91 End of Year Balance Sheet, 1931, Balance Sheets and Associated Papers, United Artists Collection (Madison, WI: Wisconsin Center for Film and Theater Research).

92 Reeves to Sydney Chaplin, 12 June 1934, CA, document 00005694.

93 Gilbert Seldes, 'A Comic Masterpiece', *New Republic*, vol. 66, 25 February 1931, pp. 46–7.

94 'Mr. Chaplin', *New Statesman and Nation*, vol. 1, 7 March 1931, p. 65.

95 Syd Silverman, '*City Lights* Review', *Variety*, 11 February 1931.

96 In 'What N.Y. Critics Said about *City Lights*' (9 February 1931, p. 5), *Film Daily* excerpted reviews from ten New York newspapers: all praised Chaplin (the 'Great Man of the Cinema' exhibits 'consummate artistry') and the film ('superb', 'genuinely hilarious', a 'dazzling pattern of comedy and pathos').

97 Alexander Bakshy, 'Charlie Chaplin Falters', *Nation*, vol. 132, 4 March 1931, pp. 260–1.

98 Flora Merrill, 'Charlie Chaplin, Master Pantomimist, Discusses Economic Principles and the Shadow Art', *Madison Journal*, 24 February 1931, AdM, Album 33.

99 For a more detailed discussion of this work and of Chaplin's political perspective in the first half of the 1930s, see Charles Maland, *Chaplin and American Culture: The Evolution of a Star Image* (Princeton: Princeton University Press, 1989), pp. 135–43.

100 On Chaplin's 1942 speeches and the hostile response to *Monsieur Verdoux*, see Maland, *Chaplin and American Culture*, pp. 186–94, 231–52.

Credits

City Lights
'a comedy romance in
pantomime'
USA 1931
©1931. Charles Chaplin

Directed by
Charles Chaplin
Written by
Charles Chaplin
Photographers
Rollie Totheroh
Gordon Pollock
Music Composed by
Charles Chaplin
Settings
Charles D. Hall

Assistant Directors
Harry Crocker
Henry Bergman
Albert Austin
Musical Direction by
Alfred Newman
Musical Arrangement by
Arthur Johnston
"La violetera" by
José Padilla

[uncredited]
Production Company
Charles Chaplin
Productions
Producer
Charles Chaplin
General Manager
Alfred Reeves
Script Supervisor
Della Steele
Casting
Al Ernest Garcia

Camera Operator
Mark Marklatt
Gaffer
Frank Testera
Stills Photographer
Ralph Barton
Editor
Charles Chaplin
Sound Supervisor
Theodore Reed
Director of Publicity
Carlyle Robinson
Unit Publicist
Harry Crocker

CAST
Charlie Chaplin
a tramp
Virginia Cherrill
a blind girl
Florence Lee
her grandmother
Harry Myers
an eccentric millionaire
Allan Garcia
his butler
Hank Mann
a prizefighter

uncredited cast
Henry Bergman
janitor/official
Albert Austin
street cleaner/burglar
Joe Van Meter
burglar
Stanhope Wheatcroft
distinguished man in
café
John Rand
old tramp

James Donnelly
foreman
Eddie Baker
referee
Robert Parrish
Austen Jewell
newsboys
Tiny Ward
man on lift
Leila McIntyre
flower shop assistant
Harry Ayers
cop
Florence Wicks
woman who sits on cigar
Tom Dempsey
Victor Alexander
Eddie McAuliffe
Willie Keeler
boxers
Jean Harlow
extra in nightclub scene

In Black and White

In production between
December 1927 and 1930
Filmed in San Francisco
(California, USA).

US distributor: United
Artists Corporation
(Los Angeles premiere on
30 January 1931,
New York premiere on
6 February 1931, general
release on 7 March 1931).

Running time:
87 minutes

UK distributor: United
Artists Corporation Ltd.
(released in London on
27 February 1931).
Running time:
87 minutes 52 seconds

Copyright renewed in
1958 © The Roy Export
Company Establishment

Press materials add Mark
Marlatt's name to the list
of Photographers, Carlyle
Robinson as Director of
Publicity and Alfred
Reeves as General
Manager however none
of these name appear
onscreen.

Credits compiled by
Julian Grainger

Bibliography

Agee, James, *Film Writing and Selected Journalism* (New York: The Library of America, 2005).

Bakshy, Alexander, 'Charlie Chaplin Falters', *Nation*, vol. 132, 4 March 1931, pp. 260–1.

Bengston, John, *Silent Traces: Discovering Early Hollywood through the Films of Charlie Chaplin* (Santa Monica: Santa Monica Press, 2006).

Bordwell, David, and Kristin Thompson, *Film Art: An Introduction*, 6th edn. (New York: McGraw-Hill, 2001).

Brock, Timothy, 'The Intimate Score of the Tramp-Composer: Restoring Music for *City Lights*', in *Prima della rivoluzione: il sogno di una cosa* (Bologna: Le Mani, 2004).

Chaplin, Charles, *City Lights*, Mk2 DVD, #37648 (Warner Bros., 2003).

———, *A Comedian Sees the World/Il comico vede il mondo*, Lisa Stein (ed.) (Genoa: Le Mani, 2006).

———, *My Autobiography* (New York: Simon and Schuster, 1964).

———, 'Pantomime and Comedy', *New York Times* Section VIII, 25 January 1931, p. 6.

Chaplin, Lita Grey, and Jeffrey Vance, *Wife of the Life of the Party* (Lanham, MD: Scarecrow Press, 1998).

Cooke, Alistair, *Six Men* (New York: Knopf, 1977).

Crafton, Donald, *The Talkies: American Cinema's Transition to Sound, 1926–1931* (New York: Charles Scribner's Sons, 1997).

Crocker, Harry, 'Charlie Chaplin: Man and Mime', unpublished manuscript (Beverly Hills, CA: Margaret Herrick Library, AMPAS, 1953).

Finler, Joel, *The Hollywood Story* (New York: Crown, 1988).

Kelly, Arthur, *Letter* (Cineteca di Bologna, 1930).

Kerr, Walter, *The Silent Clowns* (New York: Knopf, 1975).

Kisch, Egon Erwin, compiled by Harold B. Segel, 'Working with Charlie Chaplin', in *Egon Erwin Kisch, the Raging Reporter: A Bio-Anthology* (West Lafayette, IN: Purdue University Press, 1997), pp. 248–60.

Kuriyama, Constance Brown, 'Chaplin's Impure Comedy: The Art of Survival', *Film Quarterly*, vol. 45 no. 3, Spring 1992, pp. 26–38.

Lynn, Kenneth, *Charlie Chaplin and His Times* (New York: Simon and Schuster, 1997).

Maland, Charles, *Chaplin and American Culture: The Evolution of a Star Image* (Princeton: Princeton University Press, 1989).

Mast, Gerald, *The Comic Mind: Comedy and the Movies*, 2nd edn. (Chicago: University of Chicago Press, 1979).

McGuirk, Charles J., 'Chaplinitis', *Motion Picture Magazine*, vol. 9 nos. 6–7, July–August 1915, pp. 85–9, 121–4.

Meryman, Richard, 'Ageless Master's Anatomy of Comedy: Chaplin, an Interview', in Kevin H. Hayes (ed.), *Charlie Chaplin: Interviews* (Jackson: University of Mississippi Press, 2005), pp. 129–41.

Molyneaux, Gerard, *Charles Chaplin's 'City Lights': Its Production and Dialectical Structure* (New York: Garland, 1983).

'Mr Chaplin', *New Statesman and Nation*, vol. 1, 7 March 1931, pp. 65–6.

Parrish, Robert, 'An Article on Charlie
    Chaplin', Chaplin Archive,
    document 00004680, 1989.
Robinson, David, *Chaplin: His Life and Art*
    (New York: McGraw-Hill, 1985).
Seldes, Gilbert, 'A Comic Masterpiece',
    New Republic, vol. 66, 25 February
    1931, pp. 46–7.
Sherwood, Robert, 'Review of *A Woman
    of Paris*', in Anthony Slide (ed.),
    Selected Film Criticism, 1921–1930
    (Metuchen, NJ: Scarecrow Press,
    1982), p. 318.
Silverman, Syd, '*City Lights* Review',
    Variety, 11 February 1931.
Vance, Jeffrey, *Chaplin: Genius of the
    Cinema* (New York: Harry N. Abrams,
    2003).
Weales, Gerald, *Canned Goods as Caviar:
    American Film Comedy in the 1930s*
    (Chicago: University of Chicago
    Press, 1985).
Young, Stark, 'Dear Mr Chaplin', *New
    Republic*, vol. 31, 23 August 1922,
    pp. 358–9.